Praise for

MW00577027

"This practical book is the missing manual for new leaders who want to become the kind of leaders they've loved— or wished they'd had. Jeff Gibbard shows us that the answer lies in being a part of your team, not above them."

TAMSEN WEBSTER, author, *Find Your Red Thread*

"*The Lovable Leader* is the leadership book that we really need. Not only does it address the responsibilities of leadership such as goal setting and strategy, but it also provides clear instructions about how to manage people, not as tools of the organization but as individuals worthy of care and respect. It's the handbook every new manager should have on their desk."

DORIE CLARK, *Wall Street Journal* bestselling author, *The Long Game*; executive education faculty, Duke University Fuqua School of Business

"Part hug, part master class, and part kick in the pants, *The Lovable Leader* is the only book new managers and aspiring leaders will ever need to up their game. If you're serious about becoming a future leader who rocks hard and with heart, RUN and get it today!"

LESLIE EHM, *Wall Street Journal* and USA *Today* bestselling author, *Swagger*

"In business, we've been debating how to get people motivated, how to keep teams connected, and how we can grow our business in a more human and sustainable way. Jeff Gibbard brings it all together in *The Lovable Leader*. Are trust, respect, and kindness the future skills that will separate the good from great brands? Let's hope so."

MITCH JOEL, author, *Six Pixels of Separation* and CTRL ALT *Delete*

"For new managers, it's like having a personal go-to coach to help you and your teams reach your highest potential. *The Lovable Leader* isn't just a book you'll read, but an actionable guide filled with frameworks, wisdom, practical advice, and heart."

ANGELA CHEE, keynote speaker; communication coach; host, *The Power of the Only* podcast

"Our society is in desperate need of new models of leadership, and *The Lovable Leader* is an incredible guide for emerging or current leaders to reach their fullest potential. It provides clear values, communication tips, conflict resolution scripts, and digestible psychology to create the care, trust, safety, and inclusion that's the glue for creating work environments where we all thrive and achieve status-quo breaking goals. I recommend this book to any individual who wants to leave behind the destructive narratives of old-school leadership to become a leader people love and are inspired by, not just in title, but in practice and purpose."

CHRISTINA BLACKEN, founder and chief narrative strategist, The New Quo

"Despite what you may think, *The Lovable Leader* is not for the faint of heart. Gibbard tackles the toughest aspects of leading people and shows you how to handle them in a way that allows you to sleep at night. This is a great book for anyone in search of the missing leadership manual."

MARC A. PITMAN, CEO, The Concord Leadership Group

"Jeff Gibbard is adding a key element to the leadership conversation, growing who we are as human beings. He pulls back the veil to clear up any confusion between leadership skill and leadership behavior, and shows us the mindset change needed to become great leaders. This book is ideal for leaders who recognize that being a great leader starts with accessing what makes us great humans."

JEANETTE BRONÉE, keynote speaker; care-driven leadership and culture strategist

"*The Lovable Leader* is the book I wish every new manager read before their first day. Jeff Gibbard provides the complete set of tools that leaders need to build effective and collaborative teams, and the book is rich with both practical frameworks and clear examples. Unlike many leadership books that focus exclusively on goals and results, I appreciate how this book takes the time to highlight safety, care, trust, and inclusion as critical aspects of effective leadership."

ROBBIE SAMUELS, author, *Small List, Big Results* and *Croissants vs. Bagels*

"Jeff Gibbard hooked me within the first few pages of *The Lovable Leader* by saying, 'Be worth following.' In today's age of 'instant internet leaders' the reality of true leadership is wrapped up quite nicely in Gibbard's three pillars. If you've ever wanted to build a great team, this should be required reading as Gibbard's words not only set the tone, but also provide the path to make it so. Regardless of your leadership 'status,' being brand new to leadership or well seasoned, you will absolutely find action items that will benefit you and your team. Well done, Jeff Gibbard. Thanks for sharing your wisdom within the pages of this book."

DOUG SANDLER, CEO and podcast coach, Turnkey Podcast Production

"Jeff Gibbard's *The Lovable Leader* is a step-by-step playbook for helping new managers become the most effective leaders possible. Best of all, the plethora of lessons throughout the book are focused on how to be our best selves while leading others."

MIKE DOMITRZ, author; speaker; founder, The Center for Respect

"Great companies have never been built on 'command and control' leadership. In *The Lovable Leader*, Jeff Gibbard shows us the new way. Whether you are new to leadership or you've been leading teams for years, you need to read this book."

LAURA GASSNER OTTING, *Washington Post* bestselling author, *Limitless*

THE
LOVABLE
LEADER

THE LOVABLE LEADER

BUILD GREAT TEAMS WITH
TRUST, RESPECT, AND KINDNESS

JEFF GIBBARD

PAGE TWO

Cataloguing in publication information is
available from Library and Archives Canada.
ISBN 978-1-77458-176-6 (paperback)
ISBN 978-1-77458-177-3 (ebook)

Page Two
pagetwo.com

Edited by Kendra Ward
Copyedited by Steph VanderMeulen
Cover and interior design by Taysia Louie

jeffgibbard.com
superheroinstitute.org

To my wife, Erica, and my
daughter, and to all people who
aspire to change the world.

To Hope,

I hope you
LOVE this.
keep being Lovable!

CONTENTS

INTRODUCTION
THE CALL TO ACTION

———

IT COULD only be described as a perfect day. The sun was out, the breeze was gentle, and aside from a few big, puffy clouds, it was clear blue skies as far as the eyes could see. More importantly, there was absolutely no traffic on the road as my wife and I drove back home after a long weekend with friends in Annapolis, Maryland. I love long drives with my wife: it gives us the time to talk that we often can't find during a busy work week. We talk about all sorts of things, but on this particular drive, she was telling me about challenges she was dealing with at work. At the time, she was brand-new to a leadership role and was having issues with the team she oversaw. Because I had a decade of experience managing people, my wife asked for my advice about how to handle the situation.

She described her teammate as having a negative attitude—he couldn't stop himself from inadvertently saying condescending and offensive things to customers and teammates alike, and his work ethic could best be described as "when I feel like it." Another teammate, although exceedingly hilarious, said completely inappropriate things at work and was routinely in conflict with other teammates. And then there was the teammate who showed up late every day, and when confronted about her performance, would burst into tears, apologize, and promptly return to the same behavior the next day.

We had talked through various aspects of motivation, conflict resolution, and leadership for more than an hour, when the outline for this book came to me. We paused our discussion to capture in Evernote what would become the training curriculum for my wife to practice.

At that time, I had been running my first agency, True Voice Media, for about five years. Over the years, my small but mighty digital marketing agency had grown to a team of ten that included both employees and contractors. Seven years after starting True Voice Media, my agency was acquired, and I became part of a five-person ownership team, with more than thirty employees and contractors spread across two cities. Suddenly, the size and complexity of my team and responsibilities multiplied, and I was forced to grow exponentially. A year and a half later, I left and launched the company I'd always dreamed of creating: The Superhero Institute, a coaching certification program with a development methodology for unlocking human potential. Now, I balance my time between writing, speaking, helping supercharge agencies, training coaches, and working as a strategy consultant for large-scale businesses.

This is all to say that I have led large teams, I have led small teams, and I have worked alone. I've worked at hundreds of companies as a consultant. I have coached people who are on my payroll and those who I send a 1099 form at the end of the year. All of this experience has given me the unique opportunity to acquire an extensive catalog of leadership principles, conflict resolution techniques, and effective conversation frameworks for a wide variety of environments and situations.

And because of these skills that I've developed, my wife has continued to use car rides, long and short, as an opportunity to ask for advice and coaching. Every morning I drive my wife to work, and we discuss the day ahead. I'm so grateful to watch as the advice and guidance I give her filters through her unique personality.

She is why this book is called *Lovable Leader*.

My wife is among the most lovable people you could ever have the pleasure of meeting. It's not just me who believes this. Scores of people would eagerly line up to describe her personality with words and phrases such as "sunshine," "a fairy-tale princess," "a warm hug," and, of course, "lovable." I tell you this because I believe that her way of being in the world is the secret ingredient we've all been looking for. It's what makes the practice of leadership come together for maximum effectiveness. It's also something that we all have access to, and in the pages ahead, you will learn how to bring it out in yourself.

My wife doesn't run NASA, and she isn't the CEO of a Fortune 100 company, but those aren't the only examples of leadership we need in this world. Untold leadership opportunities happen every single day in middle management stand-up meetings, ninety-day reviews at start-ups, and even last Wednesday at some small business in Topeka, Kansas. Inside every company are countless opportunities for leaders at all levels to do better. Leadership is not reserved for a few people at the top. It's for everyone who decides that they want to show up bigger and better at work, at home, or at an after-work flag football league.

Lovable Leader is my call to action for you—and we really need you.

Our culture of work is broken, and we can only fix it together. Leadership cannot continue to be defined primarily by its impact on the bottom line. Perpetuating that idea serves only to guide managers toward learning new, more subtle methods of manipulation to milk a little more productivity out of each cog in the machine, just so they can get a promotion.

Obviously, results matter, and in business, that means money. Now more than ever, we need leaders who think bigger than that. Leadership is the profound opportunity to be the best versions of ourselves by helping people become the best versions of themselves. It's the chance to fundamentally change how we all experience the labor that occupies our day and puts food on our tables—that is, by bringing the relationships to the forefront and creating safe environments in which to reach our potential.

Together, we can do work that is truly meaningful and that gives us a sense of purpose and connection. Today, we are reclaiming leadership, and we do it for all of us.

I'm counting on you.

Be Worth Following

The greatest leaders are fundamentally no different from you and me. They choose certain ways to behave, either through instinct or education, formal and informal. Great paragons of leadership forge new paths and bring about something remarkable, all because they have one thing in common: people are willing to follow them.

Seriously, break it down: Isn't leadership simply the act of leading others toward something? If you want be followed, you must convince and inspire others to believe that you are worth following. It's all right there in the job title.

But if you're like most leaders out there, you have a problem...

A study by Gallup found that only 15 percent of workers say they are "highly involved in and enthusiastic about their work and workplace." Furthermore, it's estimated that actively disengaged employees cost the United States $483 billion to $605 billion per year in lost productivity. So... that's not great.

Not only that, there's a widespread issue with trust. The Edelman Trust Barometer comes out every year and reports on people's feelings about trust and credibility. It has shown that trust in our traditional institutions is consistently lackluster. Whether we're talking about CEOs, experts, or traditional media, the revered gatekeepers and trust signals are now being questioned more than ever.

But that's not all! Job stress is also climbing:

The survey of nearly 2,000 professionals, conducted by Korn Ferry, also asked professionals up and down an organization about the impact workplace stress had on them. More than three-quarters of the respondents, 76%, say stress at work has had a negative impact on their personal relationships, and 66% say they have lost sleep due to work stress. A small but significant number, 16%, say they've had to quit a job due to stress.

The largest source of current stress: bosses. The survey shows 35% of the respondents say their boss is their biggest source of stress at work, and 80% say a change in leadership, such as a new direct manager or someone higher up the organizational chart, impacts their stress levels.

Study after study shows that the problem is bad and getting worse. Much of this is brought on or at least exacerbated by technology. The world is changing around us because things are moving faster than ever before.

Technology has allowed for more jobs to be performed remotely. Although this is great in some ways, it has produced a few notable consequences. Wages are driven down because less expensive global talent is available. Remote workers can also often feel isolated from their peers and disengage easily.

Employee retention has become more challenging as new technologies have opened the communication and information visibility landscape. This means that your teams can find new opportunities, that your competitors have greater access to privately communicate with your employees. Do you have what it takes to keep your best employees, or will they be lured away?

For many, leadership is just something that comes with their title. It's something they were dropped into and that they do without passion or purpose. To those people, I humbly submit that leadership is more important than an afterthought.

An employee who feels disrespected, unappreciated, or disengaged at work brings that energy home with them. In some cases, they may not have a healthy outlet for those feelings. What happens at work doesn't just stay at work. The days of compartmentalizing each aspect of our lives is rapidly eroding, because our "always-on" smartphone culture has changed the boundaries where work and life are supposed to balance. We've seen the unhealthy effects of that behavior, and although our leadership cannot solve all of the world's problems, it can help.

As a leader, you can make a safe environment for your team. You can alleviate stress rather than cause it. You can make people feel valued in the place they spend the vast majority of their waking hours each day. You can be an ethical compass and inspire your team members to be a force for good, even after they clock out.

The Case for Doing Better

I have a strong opinion about the responsibility of leadership to make the world a better place. I want your team members to feel safe. I want you to actively reduce harm in every aspect of your leadership. I want you to appreciate your impact on other people and how your interactions can fundamentally reshape the world around you. I want you to finish this book with a default operating system that leads with others' best interest in mind. All this can be accomplished without sacrificing results.

I started The Superhero Institute because I believe that

- all people are capable of extraordinary things

- our obstacles can empower us and build character instead of defining and limiting us

- our abilities combined with our choices give every person the opportunity to become a Superhero

If you read this book, you will acquire new skills to be a better leader. However, many of the skills you will learn could be used for the wrong reasons. Without a code, we can stray from the path. To guide you to use your leadership powers for good, I'd like to share with you The Superhero Code. A commitment to these ten principles will ensure that your work as a leader is ethical and directed toward safety, kindness, and fairness:

- **Responsibility:** I will use the power or privilege I currently have to make a difference. It is my responsibility to do it.

- **Protection:** I will use my resources to create safe emotional and physical spaces for others. I will take accountability and find a rectifying action if harm is caused by myself or others.

- **Self-sacrifice:** I am willing to put other peoples' needs over my self-interest for the greater good of the community or the mission I'm in service of, with boundaries for meeting my own needs in healthy and productive ways.

- **Courage:** Even when I'm scared or out of my comfort zone, I will not avoid challenges; I will confront issues.

- **Resilience:** Sometimes, I will face unexpected challenges and difficulties. I will find ways to move through these experiences and note the lessons from these moments. I will always get back up and persevere.

- **Empathy:** I will always try to understand other points of view, even if I do not agree with them, and I will challenge views that are biased or harmful to the humanity and rights of myself or others.

- **Compassion:** I will always see the humanity in others and care about their well-being.

- **Vulnerability:** My greatest source of strength comes from allowing myself to connect with those I trust by sharing my life experiences, successes, failures, feelings, and inner thoughts.

- **Honesty:** In order to help others, I must establish trust. Trust cannot grow in the absence of truth. Therefore, I will not lie; I will speak only what I know to be true.

- **Action:** In order to create real change, especially in service of these other commitments, I must take action to move beyond words and ideas.

Great leadership is a glorious balance, held together by a deep understanding of what you are trying to accomplish with the guidelines to ensure you honor the responsibilities of the role. Leadership is not an achievement, nor a destination, but rather a practice that you will adopt for life.

This is what lovable leadership is about: the aspects of leadership that require emotional intelligence, empathy, humility, compassion, and trust. Amid all other externalities, *these* are the things we can control—how we relate to one another. Leaders who care for others and who can be trusted to lead into an uncertain future are a rarity these days. How often do you hear someone rave about what they do for a living? How often do they talk about how great their manager is? Even more rare, how often do you hear someone exclaim something like, "I love my job and I trust my leadership team completely"?

What Are You Managing?

Too many managers are in their roles because they were once good at doing a particular job. As a result, they were promoted. The thinking goes that if they are good at *doing a thing*, then naturally they will be good at managing people, right?

Nothing could be further from reality.

Doing a job and managing people are almost entirely different skill sets—unless the job you were good enough to be promoted for was managing people. Too many people are promoted into leadership roles without the necessary training in how to manage people.

There are two primary reasons for this:

- The position needs to be filled, and there is neither an existing formal training program nor the time or budget allocated to providing proper training.

- The position needs to be filled, and the decision criteria is focused almost exclusively on the hard skills of the position without giving adequate weight to the learned ability of leading people.

A person promoted without adequate training is likely to become, at best, a mediocre manager of people and, more likely, someone who drives the people working for them insane. Even in the rare cases when someone has a "natural gift" for dealing with people, leadership entails far more than just personality and "people skills." Although some organizations are capable of staying afloat with mediocre managers who check the boxes and get the work done, they'll never fulfill their true potential.

The natural consequence of poor management is higher turnover, lower productivity, lesser-quality results, and a diminished quality of life experience for all team members, including the manager! In more dire circumstances, poor management can completely stall the growth of team members. Talented team members may wisely opt to stay in their current positions rather than move into a new role under a poor manager, even when that move comes with increased pay. The choice to ignore the importance of leadership training will effectively suffocate the potential of rising stars. The impact of a bad manager will be felt throughout an entire company.

Fortunately, nearly all of this can be mitigated through proper training on how to manage people, rather than just assuming job-specific knowledge will be sufficient as a stand-in for people skills.

The principles outlined in *Lovable Leader* are intended to guide you as a leader, to provide a framework you can operate from. You should be reading this book if:

- You have just moved into a leadership role and need to understand where to devote your time and attention.

- You need to understand how to manage different personality types.

- You need to be able to set goals and hold people accountable for realizing those goals.

- You want to be respected and taken seriously by both your team members and your supervisors.

Chances are you've been dropped into this new role without any training in management and leadership skills. You've had little training in effective communication. You've had to quickly establish working relationships while being accountable for results. No one has told you how to manage this new stress of leadership. No one has advised you about conflict resolution, setting boundaries, self-care, or any other aspect of this new role.

For you, I offer this straightforward handbook that provides all of the guidance traditionally missing from a new manager's orientation. This handbook has simple, easy-to-follow frameworks for succeeding and thriving in a leadership role. This advice is ethical and scalable. This framework is designed to foster loyalty and grow cohesive and collaborative teams. For those who embrace these concepts, work will never look the same again. No obstacle will seem insurmountable, no conflict too difficult to resolve. No interaction will lack respect. Even when things don't work out, everyone will walk away better off than if you had not read this book in the first place.

You will become the kind of leader people follow from company to company, for whom they may even quit their current job. You will inspire people to dream bigger, and you will have the skills to ensure those dreams become a reality. This is for those who are ready to go from uncertain to empowered and from overlooked to revered.

If that is you, then I want you to know you were born to be a leader. I'm glad you're here.

Now, if you're ready... let's dive in.

THE LOVABLE
LEADERSHIP MINDSET

Lovable leadership begins when you adopt a particular mindset. This style of leadership is grounded, real, and profoundly simple. Once you understand this, all that remains is a choice and the practice. Mindset is the start of your journey. Welcome.

The Three Lenses of Leadership

Whether you are a tyrant, an angel, or a lovable leader, the path of leadership will never be easy. The principles outlined in this book will be difficult at times. You will struggle against your deeply ingrained instincts and habits. This is why it is important for you to understand this fact right now. Leadership is your *responsibility*, your *burden*, and your *privilege*.

It is your *responsibility* because the decision to be a leader means that you feel "the calling." You know that if you can make a difference, you must make a difference. If you have the skills to help your team, it is your responsibility to offer those skills. It is your responsibility as a leader to protect, grow, and support your team. The responsibility is assigned to you the day you call yourself a leader, and the day you willingly avoid that responsibility, you lose the right to call yourself a leader. It's part of the job; wear your responsibility as part of your uniform. Make it a central theme of your code.

It is your *burden* because leadership is hard. It requires you to attend to more, to carry a greater share of the work, and to be the first to step in to help when needed. Leadership can mean putting the entire team on your back at times and carrying them through challenges and uncertainty. This burden is the price of privilege. You should be joyful for the opportunity to carry it.

It is your *privilege* because you are not owed loyalty, deference, or someone else's labor. It is your privilege because while everyone can exhibit leadership traits, teams will often look to one leader. Therefore, if that is you, the privilege and advantages that this role affords you are not to be taken for granted. You should always honor this privilege by seeking to earn it, day after day.

Many people will spend a lifetime fighting tooth and nail to be heard and acknowledged. They stand up and scream, demanding to be counted and for their voice to be heard. If you find yourself in a position where people look to you, trusting you, charging you with protecting and leading them, then that is a privilege, and it comes with the job. You must also assume the many responsibilities of your role and understand that at times it may feel like a burden.

Leadership is *always* all three qualities at once. When it is a responsibility, it is often a burden. When it is your privilege, it is also your responsibility. You often deal with the burden because of the privilege of leadership and the responsibilities that come with it. These are the realities of leadership, and I strongly recommend you think about this perspective until you can wholeheartedly adopt it.

That was the short way of explaining it. Let's go a little deeper.

Leadership is your responsibility

The word "responsibility" can mentally conjure all sorts of images. For example, think about what it meant when your parents used it. Perhaps they were talking about driving safely or being careful not to drink too much. In this context, responsibility means cautious, smart, and mature.

Think about how you've used the word on your résumé or LinkedIn profile. In this context, it's more like "results directly attributable to" or "stuff I watched over to make sure nothing caught on fire." Perhaps it's just another way of saying, "It was one of my jobs."

In this context, I'm using the word "responsibility" in a larger and potentially more aspirational context. At a high level, I believe that leaders should adhere to deontological ethics, sometimes referred to as "duty ethics." If that sounds a little heavy, you may be more familiar with another example.

Stan Lee, the creator of Spider-Man, wrote: "With great power there must also come—great responsibility!" The quote's origin predates Uncle Ben by several hundred years, making appearances in the Christian Bible, the French Revolution, and a litany of other speeches and writings. However, since I'm a *major* Spider-Man fan, I'm choosing to cite the more popular usage in *Amazing Fantasy* no. 15 from 1962.

Though many people have heard that quote, what some may not know is why it is so important to the philosophy/ethos of Spider-Man. For those who have seen any of the movies or read any of the old comics, I'll be brief.

Shortly after acquiring his super-abilities, Peter Parker has the opportunity to stop a crime from happening, yet he chooses not to. His justification for inaction in many versions of the story is that the criminal is in the act of taking advantage of a person who had just taken advantage of Peter himself. So, even though he has the strength, speed, agility, and stamina to easily thwart this crime, Peter lets the criminal go, savors a small sense of schadenfreude, and goes about his evening. The criminal then murders Peter's Uncle Ben.

This is the birth of Spider-Man—the vigilante, crime-stopping hero. Peter had the power to do the right thing and stop bad things from happening. And in that moment, he chose not to. Then, that decision came back to hurt him personally. His guilt ignited something inside him that left him no other option than to accept his responsibility to use his power to do whatever he could to stop others from feeling that pain.

Heavy stuff, right?

This entire scenario and the resultant worldview captures the spirit of deontological ethics, which is the "theory that the morality of an action should be based on whether that action itself is right or wrong under a series of rules, rather than based on the consequences of the action." Doing the right thing simply because it is the right thing to do is a good basis for most of your leadership decisions.

That said, you are responsible for more than just your intent. You are also responsible for your impact. Your best intentions don't negate the harm that well-intended actions may have. You are also responsible for how you treat each person on your team, for how your actions directly or indirectly affect your team, and for what you tolerate. If someone can't sleep because of what went on under your care, that's on you.

Responsibility is a pact you make with yourself and, if you're willing to go one step further, with the world. No one asks this of you. You demand it of yourself because you choose to see doing the right thing as your responsibility, since you have the power to impact others. You have special talents. You are *you*, and there is no one else like you out there. Just you. You determine who you are and who you will become.

This responsibility should pull at you and stretch you. It should motivate you to make the biggest possible impact you believe yourself capable of. When you choose to become the best possible version of yourself, then you know in your heart that you must lead. Because waiting around for the permission that you are "allowed to lead" is not an option, and waiting around for instructions is even worse.

That is what I mean by responsibility. *That* is the mindset of a lovable leader.

Leadership is your burden

At the risk of alienating my less geeky readers, I'm going to make a few more Spider-Man references throughout this chapter. Bear with me. I promise they'll all make sense.

In Spider-Man fandom and internet meme culture, there is something that is often referred to as "Parker Luck." In the comics, despite choosing to do the right thing, Peter Parker is chronically stuck in a series of situations in which the right thing is the most difficult option; he generally negatively impacts his own life at the expense of making the world safer. This is the other side of deontological ethics—sometimes, the outcome of doing the right thing *should* be considered.

Peter's relationships are a mess, he's constantly in danger of failing his classes, and even though he's a genius scientist, his job of staying up all night to stop crime often leaves him too exhausted to show up to work on time or hold down a job.

The role of a leader often requires sacrifices. You are often the one who suffers most. Responsibility is a weight you carry for others. Your strength in all areas requires you to look out for those who need you and step up to challenges. You may also have to step aside from a challenge. It is not your job to be your team's savior. You are not a knight in shining armor. You are not superior to your team. You are just someone with a leadership mindset who is willing to endure the pressure so that the entire team can flourish. Part of that burden is the sacrifice of your ego's desire to be a hero, to get the accolades and adoration.

You do this and think like this because leaders must.

Leadership is not easy—you will be challenged, you will become tired, you will want to give up. You will want to take over, you will want to lash out at times... but as a leader you remain steady and move forward. You will make mistakes, and you will need to own them. That can be a heavy burden for anyone. But this is a burden you should be honored to carry despite the weight of the responsibility and expectations.

Leadership is the burden you take on because you know that someone must. And since you also know that leadership is your responsibility, you carry that burden.

If leadership were easy, everyone would want to do it and be good at it. But it's not, they don't, and they aren't.

It's a burden to sacrifice your ego. It's a burden to constantly check yourself.

Leadership is your privilege

Perhaps you were asked to lead. Perhaps you were dropped into it. Perhaps you asked for it.

Congratulations. In each of those scenarios, you have an incredible opportunity with clear benefits. Leadership affords you a great number of advantages that others may not have access to. Leadership roles come with additional benefits such as salary or equity. They have an implied authority, and while lovable leadership philosophy does not lean on that fact, acknowledging it is important. Leadership also gets you a seat at the table, the chance to contribute to or directly make decisions of consequence. In many cases, leaders are less likely to be replaced than the team's rank-and-file members. All of these are privileges—special rights or advantages, available only to a particular person or group.

Being a leader means that you have a unique chance to show how you wield the tools of authority, power, and control. You can shine by showcasing how you set goals, design strategy, and manage your team. These choices define you as a leader. The opportunity to make them is a privilege.

Privilege does not mean to imply that you didn't work hard. However, in some cases, considering whether your path to a leadership role was made easier because of your race, gender, class, family, or connections is important. In those cases, own your luck, acknowledge that privilege, and honor it by using your position to dismantle the systems of power that systematically benefit some over others.

No matter what circumstances you were born into, you are not entitled to be a leader. Leadership is not a title; it's a mindset and a way of behaving. Regardless of your title or implied authority, you are a true leader only if someone is willing to be led by you.

Once you are in a leadership position, acknowledge the many benefits that come with it, embrace those advantages, and honor the opportunities that it presents to you.

Honoring your role as the leader and the many privileges it affords you means that you must earn it day in, day out.

Choose Leadership

Are you a leader? This is a simple question, but no online quiz will help you answer it. There is no right answer to it. You just have to choose.

Whether you work for a company or for yourself, whether you have a leadership title or not, is irrelevant. Being a leader is not about a job title. It is a mindset.

Now, understand there's a big difference between being *a leader* and being *the boss*. In my world, the "B-word" is forbidden. We just don't use it, and I take it as an insult if someone applies it to me. Seriously, just think about how the word "boss" even makes you feel. In my experience, the boss

- draws their authority from their title

- makes unilateral decisions instead of involving their team

- places blame on others rather than accountability on themselves

- communicates hierarchy instead of unity

- is the reason good people leave

If you do not consciously decide to be a leader, you are just someone with a title, and you'll probably wind up becoming nothing more than someone's "boss."

You can lead in any area of life with a leadership mindset, which will guide you regardless of whether your team is made up of employees, friends, or strangers.

So, before you go any further, you must answer this two-part question: Will you take the easy way out and be a "boss" or are you ready to fully step into your role—and your life—as a leader?

Lovable Leadership

Once you've decided to be a leader, you have another choice: What kind of leader do you want to be? My obvious vote is that you choose to be lovable. The lovable leader framework is actually quite simple. There are three basic elements:

- care
- trust
- safe travels

All three of these elements are expressed through your words and actions. We'll explore these in detail in the coming chapters.

As the term implies, lovable leadership is simply the result of taking two different ideas and combining them: 1) be loving and lovable, and 2) be a leader. To be loving and lovable requires you to care about, respect, and protect your team; build strong bonds of trust; and be supportive. To be a leader requires you to be ambitious, motivate others, carry an unyielding commitment to others' growth, and align and realign your team around a desired outcome or mission.

Lovable leadership incorporates aspects of many leadership styles to create one simple framework that is profoundly human. This framework is built using the vast bodies of research on influence, trust, and human nature. Lovable leadership favors easy-to-follow guidelines that simplify the complex nature of human interactions. It is not about overcomplicated power dynamics and manipulation.

Unlike the general topic of leadership, this framework is *not* amoral. Quite the contrary, this leadership paradigm is entirely dependent on you doing the "right thing," time and time again, even when presented with an easier or more profitable route. I define the "right thing" as that which maximizes happiness and well-being for all parties, reducing harm, and achieving the best results over time.

Lovable leadership isn't some fluffy, hippie-inspired tantrum I'm throwing as a response to a system that is working beautifully. It is the leadership paradigm I feel we need to embrace in a system that is *not* working... and we need it before it is too late. It's about bringing compassion and equity into our companies and forcing these qualities to spread throughout every level—because it's the right thing to do.

The real leadership struggles that lovable leaders need to address are the daily interactions with people who do not feel heard, seen, recognized, or acknowledged. They are the people who feel disrespected, overlooked, overshadowed, and talked over. They are our team members who feel uncertain about their growth opportunities, who lack a sense of purpose in their role, and who want to feel proud of what their company is doing in the world. And if I, a white cis-male (a male born with sexual organs that match my gender identity) in this society, have experienced any of this, you can bet your ass that it is absolutely *nothing* compared to what women, LGBTQIA+, BIPOC, neurodivergent, or people with disabilities go through.

We are all in this together, and the way that our businesses operate, the behaviors we encourage, and the priorities of our leaders will not only shape next quarter's profits but will be one more vote for the type of world we want to live in.

LOVABLE LEADER'S CHEAT SHEET

To adopt the lovable leader's mindset, I will remember that:

- Leadership is a choice, not a title.

- Leadership is a practice, not a destination.

- Leadership is my responsibility, burden, and privilege.

- My leadership responsibilities include goal setting, strategy development, communication, team management, and navigating change.

- "Leader" is just another role on the team. I will stay humble and I won't be a "boss."

CARE

Care is an essential element of love. Loving anything would be difficult if you simultaneously didn't care about it. If you want people to feel safe under your leadership, if you want them to trust you, if you want them to be loyal and hardworking for a shared cause, you have to care. And when I say "care," I mean really care.

WE'RE CONDITIONED by society to dislike work or see it as a necessary evil rather than as an inspirational part of our lives. Caring about something, at least in my formative teenage years—and in my formal business education—was regarded as lame, quaint, and naive, or a sign of weakness. That callous sentiment lives at the heart of a phrase we hear too often: "It's not personal, it's business." We've created a paradigm where being professional is different from being a decent human being. I call BS on this. I don't buy the whole broken setup. It's about time we start really caring about things—taking things personally, not professionally. Distancing ourselves emotionally from outcomes is only seeking to protect ourselves from embarrassment and shame. And anyone who has seen a Brené Brown talk on shame knows that is not the ideal way to go through life.

It's time to stand up tall and be bigger than that. Leadership demands it.

You need to care deeply about your people. Consider these questions.

- Whom does it benefit if you don't really care what happens to employees outside of work? Are we really so callous that we think the only time our people should matter is when they're "on the clock"?

- When you talk to your team members, do you consider how your words and tone influence your relationships?

- Do you assume that you know someone's pronouns? A critical aspect of care is respecting people's identities.

- If you don't care about someone enough to think about what happens to them after you fire them, then did you care about them enough when you hired them?

These points are meant to suggest that you think about the *person*, not the *employee*. I'm not advocating that you call your employees on weekends to check in on them. I'm simply encouraging you to create an opening so that your team members know you are available to support them.

If you notice that one of your team members is sad, or seems "off," it is fine to be concerned. It's fine to check in on them in a caring and noninvasive way. It's kind of a jerk move to suggest they leave their personal lives at home and "be professional." When you care about your people, you are available for and interested in them while also understanding and respecting their boundaries.

Some successful organizations work well together for a short period but then begin to see the team dynamic break down. I've seen companies who let exceptionally talented people walk out the door because they didn't care enough to notice the signs that someone was dissatisfied, unchallenged, and disengaged. I had a front-row seat to see someone laid off, over the holidays, right after they'd asked about their job security before making a serious financial decision. This person also had just completed a lengthy project that would go on to earn the company money. I've even seen companies lose their most valuable team member by totally bungling time off for a death in the family. Can you even imagine? Negotiating timelines and pressing for status updates with someone who just lost a loved one?

Problems often arise when people think on short timelines or only about their own wants and needs. The easiest way to increase your level of care is to think about your relationships on a longer timeline and focus on them instead of on yourself. When you do this, you will naturally take more care with the relationship.

Even if the person you care about spends only a few days on your team, thinking about the relationship as long term and taking greater care with it will benefit you and the other person. You never know when a relationship will come back around.

A team will be successful as long as they care about the same goals and each other. If that breaks down, so too does the team. The potential for long-term success on a team increases proportional to each person's level of care for everyone else on the team.

Even if you need to remove someone from your team, do so with care. What happens to someone once you no longer employ them should matter to you. If it doesn't, then there wasn't enough diligence in hiring that person in the first place.

You also need to care about your work. How great can you be if you are only putting in a satisfactory effort? How hard will your team work if they see you "phoning it in"? How outstanding can your team be if you expect only that they get it done but not that they strive for excellence and care about the outcome? Caring about the work is a sign of your belief in the integrity of the work itself. Your loving leadership needs to include your inspiring love for what you do.

And you need to care about your organization. Hopefully you're in an organization you can be proud of. Because how extraordinary can your company or your team be if you don't care about the legacy you're building? Is this just a job, or are you trying to be legendary?

Every person at your company reflects the organization, and likewise, the organization reflects every person who works there. If you are going to work for a company, you should be willing to care about what happens there. You should be willing to fight for what is right there. You should be willing to defend your people to the company and the company to your people. You do this because you care.

It's Not About People Liking You

Before we go further, I should probably clarify what I mean when I talk about love between a leader and team members. Love means:

- That you care about your people and protect them from harm.

- That there is a strong sense of respect.

- That you have a commitment to honesty and transparency.

- That you accept people exactly as they are, without seeking to manipulate them, while supporting their growth, success, and happiness.

- That you are thoughtful about relationships over the long term, considering the impact of how you communicate and always choosing to be kind.

Let me be clear: lovable leadership is not about people liking you. No matter how much you care, not everyone is going to like you. This has always been difficult for me throughout my career, but it's true. Some people may find your personality grating. They may not like how you dress or even the pitch of your voice. They may have a host of unconscious or conscious biases against you.

Regardless, there's still room for them to love you in all the ways I described above.

That said, it certainly doesn't hurt your chances if people like you. In fact, there's a strong scientific basis for believing it has at least some importance in your ability to influence people. Robert Cialdini's seminal book *Influence: The Psychology of Persuasion* details the six "weapons of influence." One of those six is affinity. The idea that people are more likely to be influenced by those they like has been tested and validated.

However, as I mentioned, despite the obvious benefits, lovable leadership is about more than just whether people like you. You need to do a lot more than simply being nice to your people, liking them first, and avoiding situations where they might resent you. It's your job to help them grow, which means you may need to do uncomfortable things, like challenge them. In your commitment to stand for their growth and success, you have to let go of any worries about whether or not they like you.

Put Your People First

On my podcast, *Shareable*, I do a segment called "Mic Swap," where I let the guest switch places with me and become the host. One episode, my guest was Doug Sandler, host of *The Nice Guys on Business* podcast. When he switched places with me, he asked me to rank, in order of importance, these four parts of my business:

- employees
- customers
- products
- systems

Without hesitation I answered employees first. Why?

Because I know that if I build an extraordinary team, they are going to take care of our customers, and they will ensure the best service and products. It's simple. Your employees come first. In the lovable leadership framework, there is no other answer to that question.

So what does it mean to put your team first?

Stand for your people

If you want to gain your people's trust, show them that you are willing to stand up for them at every chance you get.

When a team member doesn't have to question whether you are on their side and watching out for them, they start to trust that support will be there when needed. Furthermore, when you "walk the walk" and get in the trenches with them, your people grow to trust you. When your team trusts you enough, they will not hesitate to follow you anywhere... even into battle.

By being vulnerable, authentic, and transparent, you allow your team to truly connect with you. This, in turn, opens the door for them to be open and vulnerable with you. This helps build connection and understanding, and creates the condition for open dialogue and coaching. Few people are open to coaching or guidance from someone who doesn't understand them.

Among the defining moments for any leader are those in which they have to choose whose side to take. To inspire trust and safety on your team, it is imperative that you take advantage of these opportunities to reinforce each team member's position, and to signal that you will protect them.

Standing for your people is not optional. It is not a passive afterthought. You must be on the lookout for these opportunities because if you do not come to their defense and stand for them as an ally, they will remember it.

Stand for them against outsiders

I've been in the world of client services for more than a decade. I have been part of an agency, I ran my own agency, I was on the leadership team of an agency, and even now, I work with several agencies. Agencies have clients, all sorts of them, with all manner of personalities. It should come as no surprise that, on occasion, my teams have had some difficult clients, with personalities we didn't quite mesh with. We've even been in situations where the client was upset with us, and their words and tone made that obvious. As a leader, I have often had to bear the brunt of these uncomfortable conversations. This is part of agency life.

When a client takes a negative tone with me or says something nasty, I will listen, take ownership, and give them the benefit of the doubt... up to a point, of course. But the minute a client, or anyone else, speaks down to one of my team members, I squash that crap immediately.

One team I led had a client who, because of a typo, insinuated we were "incompetent." If the client had referred to me alone, I would've calmly replied. However, when they accused my team member of being inept, I intervened immediately, stating that we did not speak to one another that way and that they would not be warned again.

Regardless of the size of a client or how much they mean to the business, there is simply no room for disrespect. If it's not something you would say to your team, never let a client say it. Your team is watching you, and it is your job to keep them safe so that they can do their best work.

Stand for them against each other

As organizations grow, the culture becomes more difficult to manage, and the complexity of intersecting human emotions grows too.

In organizations, especially large ones, there will be personality clashes. When these conflicts arise, it can be difficult not to take sides. You may have a favorite among two people who are arguing. You may recognize the implicit value to the business that one employee has above the other. You may see one employee as being right and the other as wrong. None of this is easy. There is no one method of dealing with these conflicts. But if there is one important thing to focus on when dealing with internal strife among your team, it is this: the common goal of the team.

You must acknowledge both parties in the conflict. Your commitment must be to find a resolution such that everyone on the team is willing to put down their swords in service of the larger business goal. In this way, you show that the team and its health, above any individual, are most important. You remind them that working together outweighs any single conflict. This does not mean a license to excuse bad behavior. This does not mean that you do not take corrective measures for bad behavior, bad work, or generally poor teamwork. It simply means that your primary objective is the health of the team and all of its members, followed by the accomplishment of the business goals.

By acknowledging the experience of all parties involved, you can avoid making any one person wrong and instead focus on all team members working more effectively together. Put the onus on them to learn about one another and how to best work together. Use the moment as a teaching opportunity to transform the conflict into greater connection and teamwork among your team members.

Stand for them against themselves

Believe it or not, one of your primary responsibilities as a leader is to stand for people against themselves. This is far more common than you might imagine. You may have to stand for people against themselves more often than you will against their teammates, your clients, or anyone else. All people struggle with impostor syndrome and negative self-talk at some point in their lives and careers. When a teammate is down, beating themselves up, or questioning their own abilities, your job is to be their cheerleader, the voice of positive reinforcement.

Being a leader gives you the incredible opportunity to build something larger than yourself. Your words and actions can ripple far into the future. Your leadership lessons will stay with your people long after your work together has ended and may, in turn, shape how they choose to lead.

Growing team members is among the most important aspects of leadership, and one in which I have always taken great satisfaction. Whether it is helping people acquire a new skill or working with them through a challenge, watching my team members level up has always been a joy for me. I believe that it is essential to recognize how vital your role is in helping your team grow and what an honor that is.

Remember, *it's not about you.* Helping a team member grow is about them. How you provide that support will vary. In some cases, you may need to offer hands-on mentorship, and in others, you may need to relinquish control and let your team members work through a problem on their own. Talk to them to get a sense of what they need. Ask them if they'd prefer that you take a more active role, point them toward resources to handle issues on their own, or let them handle problems entirely but support them with regular check-ins.

In some cases, a person may not know what support they require, so you'll have to make a judgment call. As long as you've included the person in the process and heard what they had to say, they should trust you. Listening to them is more effective than assuming you know best. Even if the outcome is the same as it would have been had you made a unilateral decision, including others in solving a problem is a better approach.

This is important because it affirms how you see your team members in the context of the team.

Selfless Service

Many leaders struggle because they believe their team is there to serve them. One of the most impactful changes you can make is to flip that. When you commit to serving your team members rather than expecting them to serve you, you will find that both happen anyway.

Service is a two-way street, just like trust. If you want people to do something for you, you need to do something for them. If you want people to care about you, you need to care about them. And if you're wondering why you need to go first... it's because you're a leader.

So, what does it mean to serve? A good starting place is first understanding each of your team members' goals. When you understand their objectives, you can align those with your own goals. Once you do that, helping your team members accomplish their goals also achieves the team's goals. So, what does this look like in practice?

Take this situation with Luke, for example. Luke was accountable for operations at the agency. He was working nights, weekends, and had too much to do to make an impact in any one area. As a result, the team's project management tool was long overlooked. It was painfully outdated and did little more than list the names of each client. I knew this was slowing everyone down and creating immense frustration, and as the customer experience got worse, the entire business was being put in jeopardy. The problem was, Luke was reluctant to let anyone else help.

Rather than reprimand him or reorder his priorities myself, I sought to find out what he really wanted. If I had

asked Luke, he would have said his goal was to get everything done. But that wouldn't have solved the underlying
problem, as more tasks would inevitably come across his
plate, and the team would still have no project management tool. In talking to him, it became clear that what
he really wanted was to have his nights and weekends
back, to take his lunch break daily, and to go to sleep at
a reasonable hour. This was the key to getting the project management tool overhauled in record time. If I'd
talked about him getting a new project management tool
implemented, it would've been just one more thing for
him to do, or a responsibility being ripped away from him.
Instead, we talked about getting him more of his time
back, and it started with getting a new project management tool in place so that we could see everything that
needed to be done, and reassign things to other people
so he could finally have some more balance in his life. I
offered to bring in other team members to collaborate
with Luke on the process. Once we got the goals aligned
and mobilized the team in service of one another, what
was more than a year overdue took only two months to
fix. By understanding Luke's goals, we could align our
goals with his to make progress. Luke has regained (most
of) his sanity, regularly takes lunch, and works past six
o'clock only on rare occasions.

It's important to understand that I'm not encouraging
a self-serving tactic so that you can accomplish the goals
you care about. This isn't about manipulating others so
you can get a promotion. When you care about helping
others accomplish their goals and grow, that's when you

can really make an impact. Not only will you accomplish the goals that your organization or team care about, but you will also deepen your relationship with the team members you serve. In Luke's case, I really wanted him to have a lunch break, get more sleep, get back to the gym, and bring a smile back to his face once in a while.

Yes, you must care about the goals of your organization or team. Yes, you should care about your own goals. If you want to realize both, then the best place to start is by caring deeply about your team members and their goals. When you are in service of the people on your team, you can change lives.

Show them how to behave like a leader, and inspire them to be in service of others. If you play that out in your mind, isn't that just a little bit more exciting than just helping the company make a little more money?

Be a Cheerleader and Generous with Acknowledgment

A basic principle of effective leadership is appreciating and acknowledging your people. Everyone wants to feel important. Everyone on this planet seeks acknowledgment and validation. Sure, some say they don't; but truly, validation from others, although not a great way to establish your self-worth, is an ideal way to know that your work and contributions have meaning and purpose.

In my early twenties, I read Dale Carnegie's *How to Win Friends and Influence People*. Everyone remembers something different from that book, but what stuck out for me was his writing about acknowledgment: "Remember, we all crave appreciation and recognition, and will do almost anything to get it. But nobody wants insincerity. Nobody wants flattery." Similarly, William James is quoted as saying: "The deepest principle in human nature is the craving to be appreciated."

So, if this is one of the deepest principles of human nature, why would you not appreciate your team and acknowledge their contributions? What you'll hear from great loners is an account of the many things they alone did to get where they wanted to go. What you'll hear from great leaders is what their team did to get them there.

Related to the principle of acknowledgment and appreciation is understanding that it starts with you. To engender love and respect from your team, you must love and respect them first. You must be willing to take the first step because, as the leader, you set the tone of your relationships with your team. You cannot expect someone to love and admire you if you do not create an environment in which that is a possibility by first loving them through acknowledgment and appreciation.

Be generous and sincere with your praise. When a teammate performs a task, give them credit for it and do not steal their moments.

Say please and thank you

A great article from Inc.com relates an interaction between Michael Jordan and coach Mike Krzyzewski during the 1992 Olympic Dream Team.

Here's Coach K: "It was after our first practice... and he came over and said, 'Coach, I'd like to work on some of my offensive stuff... would you please work with me?' I thought he was coming over to give me a hard time, because he's from North Carolina and I'm from Duke... and I actually think it was his way of making me feel comfortable. He said, 'Coach,' and he said, 'Please,' and when it was over, he said, 'Thanks.' He could have said, 'Hey, get over here, idiot, and work with me,' and I would have done that. I would have done it. Just like a lot of people in workplaces will do their job. But then I would have felt as inconsequential, and had no ego whatsoever, because it was stripped from me by the main guy. Instead, he gave me a chance to have an ego. He called me with respect, 'Coach,' just like knowing a person's name. He said 'please' and 'thank you'... in other words, there was no organizational chart where he was the top guy and I'm here on the bottom. It was a tremendous, tremendous thing."

Coach. Please. Thanks. Three simple words.

Three *powerful* words: words that built a bridge, established a relationship, and harnessed the power of asking for help.

Buy lunch... sometimes

This is a small one, but it can go a long way.

When you can pick up lunch for the team or buy a round of drinks, or anything else like that, you should do it. Typically, leaders make more money, or at least are believed to make more money, and buying lunch is a sign that you're willing to forego your own interests for the team's interests.

This is also, yet again, backed by research. Earlier in this chapter, I mentioned Robert Cialdini's book *Influence* and, specifically, affinity, one of the six "weapons of influence." Well, another one is reciprocity. Gifts are a way of collecting small bits of social capital by creating social debt. I'm not suggesting you do this as a means of manipulation, but rather, I want you to understand the impact that something like buying lunch can have at an unconscious level. Do it solely as a kind gesture, knowing that generous acts often enhance your ability to influence others.

LOVABLE LEADER'S CHEAT SHEET

To show my team that I care, I will...

- Make my leadership about them.

- Acknowledge and validate them.

- Be mindful of small gestures like saying thank you.

- Stand for them against outsiders, each other, and themselves.

- Serve their growth and success.

- Be their biggest cheerleader.

TRUST

*Trust is a feeling. You sense it deep in your gut. When
you trust, you allow yourself to be vulnerable.
When you trust, you feel safer taking risks. When you
trust, you can build the deep connections needed
to harmonize and align with your people.*

NOW THAT we've established that you care about your
people, your team, and your mission, let's talk about trust,
an essential part of love.

Trust is the degree to which you believe that your
expectations will be met. For instance, do you trust that if
you put an ice cube in your mouth, it will be cold? What
is your degree of confidence in that? I'm guessing, if your
ice cubes are anything like the ones that I've known, your
degree of confidence is somewhere around 100 percent.

Why? Why do you trust that ice cubes will be cold?
Does it have to do with consistency? Is your experience
with ice cubes that they are consistently cold?

To build trust, you must be consistent. This way, people know what to expect from you and thus will be highly confident that their expectations will be met. Hence, they will trust you.

Trust is a feeling you sense deep in your gut. The feeling is similar to certainty. Thus, the greater your degree of trust, the greater your degree of certainty. When someone consistently meets your expectations, that leads to certainty, through which you develop a sense of trust in an outcome. As a leader, consistency sets the expectations of your team. If you consistently blow up when things go wrong, then your team begins to expect that. If you are consistently genuine, caring, and empathetic when things go sideways, then people expect you to respond in this manner when issues arise. If you consistently exhibit care in your team members' growth, they will come to trust that your care is more than just words.

Achieving consistency requires patience. You cannot establish a reputation for consistency on day one; you have no track record. In the beginning, you can only set expectations. Day in, day out, you'll need to reinforce those expectations through your words and actions. If you do this, your people will come to trust you.

Take the time, do the work every day. People have to trust that you

- know what you're doing
- mean the words you speak
- will help them achieve their goals
- will protect them from outsiders
- will keep them safe

Without trust, your team will be weak. With mistrust, your team members will leave at the first opportunity. If you do not earn their trust, the people you are trying to lead will never follow you.

Trust also creates the conditions for valuable, useful, and actionable feedback. Even with good intentions and well-thought-out plans, you still need a critical feedback loop, and you will never get that if people lack the trust needed to give you honest feedback. So, let's look at how to build trust.

Sit on the Same Side of the Table

The *most* important framework I can offer you is this: sit on the same side of the table. You can lead a team only if you're on the team.

Pay attention. This could be perhaps the most important, useful, and practical point in this book. "Sitting on the same side of the table" is a metaphor for how you position yourself in conversations with team members. This technique is meant to align you and a colleague in a conversation that places both of you on solid, stable, and equal footing, facing the same direction. It removes defensiveness and creates a tone of collaboration and partnership by speaking to common goals. Sitting on the same side of the table is about engaging one of your most important human attributes.

I'll explain...

On my podcast, *Shareable*, I used to ask all of my guests: What is the most important skill of the future? In numerous episodes, by a wide margin, the number one answer was empathy. This was so far and away the top answer that I began applying the condition that guests had to choose a different word.

For the uninitiated, empathy is a tool to deeply connect with other human beings and living things. It is what helps deepen our understanding of each other and ourselves. It is the practice of attempting to experience something through someone else's perspective. It is listening to another's lived experience and using that to see through their eyes and hear through their ears. It is a practice of getting out of our own head and seeing reality from a different angle to expand how we process the world around us. And empathy is a (not so) secret weapon. Almost all humans can access this amazing tool, yet far too many forget to use it.

Lovable leaders foster an environment of empathy and respect in their organizations—these qualities build resiliency. Environments of empathy and respect quickly bounce back from failure and emerge stronger than before. Empathy allows you to be flexible in the face of setbacks rather than holding firm to your rigid beliefs, so that you can find new solutions. Used as a consistent framework, empathy allows your employees and teammates the space to work through problems that are holding them back.

You need empathy to help someone else grow, to help your team play more cohesively, and to form a strong bond with your team. Empathy is your most important tool. Guard it. Use it. Treasure it. Never lose it. Empathy is foundational in communicating to your team that you are not only with them but one of them.

With that in mind, here are the six actions you take to sit on the same side of the table.

Set the Table

When you set the table properly, it becomes clear that you are both sitting on the same side of it.

There are two elements of setting the table: 1) framing the conversation, and 2) identifying everyone's goals and creating alignment.

In any conversation, but especially if you need to have a difficult conversation with someone, start by setting expectations, adjusting the frame with which they process the conversation, and gaining their consent to continue. For negative conversations, I call this "softening the defenses." Prime the other person for the emotional response they are likely to experience. This limits unpredictable emotional responses.

People tend to react better when they are prepared for a conversation because, with very few exceptions, people don't appreciate being blindsided in a conversation.

Here's an example of how you might do this.

Let's say, for instance, one of your teammates has been slacking. For weeks, you've been asking for a particular assignment, and despite their assurances, they have not even started it. Under normal circumstances, an untrained leader might apply pressure with an underlying tone that is intended to elicit a fear response. However, as a lovable leader, you know that this is not the best approach for building a long-term, productive relation-ship with your team member. You also know that, aside from the impact it would have on your relationship, peo-ple are far more likely to respond positively when you respect them enough to prepare them for an honest, if tough, conversation.

So, instead of springing a conversation on them, even one that they know is coming, you soften their defenses to ensure that they are ready for it. You might say:

> Hi, I asked you to have this one-on-one conversation because we need to talk about that assignment. I know conversations like this can be uncomfortable and, as we talk, you may feel defensive at some points. I just want you to know that my intention is not to reprimand you. I want to better understand why it's not done with-out assuming anything beforehand, so that, together, we can figure out how to avoid things like this in the future. Is now a good time for us to talk about that?

An opening statement like this accomplishes two things: First, it preemptively addresses any emotions that may come up. Acknowledging the likelihood of these emotions provides validation should they arise. It also may trigger a more mindful awareness of how they are feeling that may temper their reaction to those emotions. Second, this statement clarifies your goals and intentions for the conversation. You change how the other person perceives what you are saying by framing the conversation around a desired outcome. Ideally, it dispels any presumptions the other person may have about your meaning or intention.

Now that you've explained your goals, the next part of setting the table requires you to attempt to align your goals with theirs.

In general, people tend to be much more interested in fulfilling their own goals and potential than in working to accomplish yours. As we talked about earlier, good leaders find the overlap between their goals for the team and what their team members want, personally and professionally. If you can uncover that and speak to how your goals align with theirs, you will have a much greater chance of influencing them.

This is an exercise in finding common ground. Before you attempt a productive conversation from the same side of the table, you must first understand where you both seek to go together.

While this must happen within the conversation, it's also a good idea to take the time, in advance, to sit down with each team member to understand their personal and professional goals. Pay attention to what they hope to accomplish. As I've maintained, it is your job to grow members of your team. Do the work on the front end so that you clearly understand each of your team member's goals so that you are sufficiently ready for any conversations you need to have later on.

Listen

In any situation, especially when there is disagreement or corrective action required, you need to gather information. Therefore, your next step in sitting on the same side of the table after setting it is to collect both factual data and, potentially more importantly, the perspective and emotional response of the other person. Nothing in life, or in business, is purely logical and rational. Human beings are emotional creatures and, therefore, many of our decisions are the product of an emotional response.

While your first instinct may be to jump right into talking about solutions, you must not skip this step. You're going to need to hear their side first and it will require you to listen closely. As you are listening, you must: 1) convey that you are present, listening to their words, and seeking to understand them; and 2) actually hear what they're saying and confirm that you understand what they are trying to communicate.

This is active listening, and it may take some time to master. It requires you to focus exclusively on another, without interrupting them, correcting them, or getting distracted by a smartphone buzzing in your pocket.

When actively listening, you refrain from interfering as they explain their perspective; you find the appropriate window to ask relevant follow-up questions, without judgment, and with the intention to better understand exactly what they mean.

Active listening also involves understanding the importance of body language:

- Are you giving the impression that you are interested? (Are you making eye contact; are your arms crossed, or are you leaning in; are you nodding your head or smiling?)

- Do you appear bored? (Is your expression blank; are you slouching; do you keep checking your phone or watch?)

- Do your facial features communicate a lack of belief? (Are you smirking, raising an eyebrow... did you just roll your eyes?)

Active listening is an exercise in ensuring another person feels truly heard and understood.

Tip: Use playbacks and callbacks. I use a technique that I call the "playback." There are several other names for this technique—the two most common are "mirroring" and "reflecting." I learned about playbacks and callbacks many years ago, and teach these techniques regularly as they are incredibly powerful tools. In the playback technique, you repeat the last words a person says to you and typically reframe them as a question. For example:

Team member: "Sometimes I feel as though no one listens to me."

You: "No one listens to you?"

This technique has multiple benefits. One is that it signals you listened. Rather than allowing their words to float into the ether without a response, you actively close an open loop for the other person. Another benefit is that you must listen closely so that you can repeat what the other person said. Saying the words out loud further solidifies their experience in your own mind, so you're less likely to misquote or misunderstand them.

A third benefit is that this technique prompts people to keep talking. For example:

Team member: "Sometimes I feel as though no one listens to me."

You: "No one listens to you?"

Team member: "Yes, for example, there was this one time last week when… " (Here, they will proceed to explain their thoughts and feelings, giving you the opportunity to better understand their experience.)

Use this technique to improve your active listening skills, especially when you don't fully understand what a person means by something. Playbacks make you a better listener and let the other person know that you are giving them your full attention, which in today's distracted world is a true gift.

To fully realize the benefit of the playback, you can turn it into a callback. These are widely used in comedy. The essential idea is that, toward the end of a set, a comedian tells a joke that refers to one told earlier in the set—to build a sense of rapport, a familiar in-feeling, with the audience. In the context of active listening, you call back to something the other person said earlier in the conversation or, better yet, at an earlier date. Playbacks let people know that you heard what they just said. Callbacks signal more substantial listening—that you heard what they said, remembered it, and could recall it, which gives it more gravity.

For instance:

Team member: "I think things are going really well with this client. They seem to understand our process, and I think they're going to be impressed when we send them this deliverable."

You: "That's great. I remember that the last time we spoke, you mentioned that sometimes you feel as though people don't listen to you. I'm sure that this feels very rewarding since the client is so clearly dialed in and obviously heard you loud and clear."

Use playbacks and callbacks to communicate that you are listening and that you have a pattern of being a good listener. This shows others that talking to you is of consequence, that you care.

Practice curiosity

There are few objective and absolute truths in this world. Even things that are factually provable by science can often be seen from another angle. Although we could surely debate the importance of coming to a singular agreement over the objective realities of climate change, that the Earth is a sphere, or whether evolution or intelligent design should be the dominant theory taught in schools, there is little doubt that an open mind is valuable in the context of leadership.

As humans, we tend to interpret events and assign truth to them. But someone else can view the same event and interpret it from a completely different perspective.

They, too, assign truth to it in their minds.

Many disagreements escalate and issues remain unresolved in the clash between two people's perceived truths.

If your goal in leadership is to be right, all you need to do is go on believing that your perception is the truth and reality will be quite simple. But this approach builds neither trust nor loyalty, and it certainly doesn't make a lovable leader.

Great leaders constantly question their own perspective, and refrain from assuming what people mean or what their intentions may be. Great leaders see everything in shades of gray. A willingness to be wrong makes you quicker to forgive and better at connecting with your team. The secret to unlocking this mindset is to practice curiosity. Genuine curiosity is the antidote to a closed mind, because it requires you to be intensely interested in learning something that you did not know. This will help prevent you from getting stuck on what you already know, or assuming you already know everything you need to know.

Tip: Start by asking yourself, What happened?! When something occurs, all we can be sure of is that it happened. What it was is a matter of perspective. This applies to virtually any situation in business. For instance, a team member could be late in delivering an assignment, two team members could disagree and each perceive the other as rude, or a business unit could consistently fail to deliver high-quality work. As a lovable leader, rather than yelling or scolding or disciplining, your first steps will always be to understand how the other people involved perceived the event or why they think it occurred. Ask questions and keep an open mind. Once you think you understand the other perspectives, repeat them back to ensure that you are correct. If they agree, move forward; if not, continue fact-finding until it is mutually established that you fully understand.

Going further, do everything you can to ensure that you do not unfairly shape your fact-finding mission and decisions with unconscious biases. We all have theses as a result of our upbringing, experiences, media consumption habits, and more. If you and your team have not gone through unconscious bias training to become more aware of how a person's decision-making can be unintentionally distorted, then I highly suggest it as a positive step. Aspire to look at things with an open mind and consider your own perspective. If you assume that you are right and definitively see things clearly, you're not being helpful to your team.

Once you understand their position and have demonstrated that to them, you will have shown that you care enough to hear their side. Let their perspective inform your own; then explain your perspective to them. This will reframe the conversation around the factors that are important to everyone involved.

Validate (instead of judge)

People mess up; everyone makes mistakes. But if you accuse someone of being wrong, you will immediately put them on the defensive. No one wants to be wrong. So, even when someone does something incorrectly, be careful about how you frame the conversation about it. One of the most effective techniques I've learned to diffuse a person's natural defensiveness is what I call "disarming."

Disarming means removing any implication that someone is wrong. Do this by giving people the space to be wrong without telling them they messed up. You do this by changing what you focus on. Rather than judging what they said or did as right or wrong, you focus on understanding their feelings about it and their explanation. You are not necessarily agreeing with it, supporting it, or endorsing it... you are acknowledging it, understanding it, and validating it.

You still hold people accountable. You instill a sense that they are responsible for their work. But you do not invalidate their experience or put them in a defensive position.

Let's look at a scenario. Imagine that, on Monday, I'd asked Joe for a report by Thursday morning. It's now Thursday afternoon. What if I led with a flinty judgment:

"Joe, why haven't you sent me the report I asked you for on Monday? It's late."

My tone indicates that there can be no good reason for such an error and that Joe is a bad worker. I'm insinuating that he is irresponsible. He is now thinking about the consequences of his inaction. He's potentially in a state of fear. But imagine my embarrassment if Joe had sent the report earlier in the day and I hadn't seen it in my inbox yet. I'm embarrassed, but beyond that, Joe now thinks I'm an idiot who accuses people before checking my email. I lose some of his respect. The bottom line:

Ambushing Joe with an accusation backfires whether he's done the work or not.

Now, imagine if instead I say: "Hey, Joe, when you have a moment, will you send me an update on the status of the report we talked about?"

Here, I imply that I trust Joe, and I give him the opportunity to provide an update. If he hasn't done his work, I haven't accused him, but he knows that he hasn't fulfilled his responsibility. He might give me a legitimate reason for the delay, in which case, Joe wouldn't be wrong for not sending the report. We all know business doesn't always go according to plan. So, it's important to leave room for unforeseen circumstances. If he provides a weak excuse, that would create an opening to talk about priorities in a productive manner:

Joe: "Oh, sorry, I'm a bit behind on my work. I've had some family issues I'm dealing with."

You: "Sorry to hear that, Joe. That's rough. Family issues can definitely take anyone's head out of it. Are you okay?"

Joe: "Yeah, I'm okay. Thanks for asking. I'll get that report to you this afternoon."

You: "Thanks, Joe. If anything else comes up for you, please let me know so I can help out or get you additional support. We've got to have each other's backs and, so long as I know what's on your plate, I can step in to help. Just give me the heads-up ahead of time. Sound good?"

Joe: "Sure, I'm sorry about that. Next time I'll communicate earlier."

This scenario is just one example of validating instead of judging your people. There are many ways of doing this, and you may take some time to master the subtlety involved. You will need to put yourself in someone else's shoes and consider how your words might make them feel. Over time, and with practice, you will do this quickly, in your head, right before speaking. You will train yourself to notice when you say things that indicate someone was wrong, and you will consciously remove that language from your conversations.

Align

By now you've set the stage to introduce or co-create a solution. You have set up the conditions for a productive conversation with context and goals, listened to their perspective, and validated their experience. You should be firmly sitting on the same side of the table looking in the same direction toward solutions.

Now is where you want to talk through a solution that aligns your goals with their goals. If their goal is to get a promotion and yours is to get that report, make sure to weave these two goals together into a unified solution.

Once you've presented that solution, you can move onto the final step in the process.

Close the loop

You cannot get buy-in without consent. In any conversation where you are proposing solutions, requests, or changes, you must get consent at the beginning, and then again at the end of the conversation.

These are important steps that empower the other person within the conversation rather than making them a bystander. By getting their consent and genuine buy-in at the beginning of the conversation, you create receptivity. By doing it at the end, you create accountability and close the loop.

Both initial consent and closing the loop at the end are accomplished by posing a question that offers a choice: Does that sound reasonable? Does this work for you? Are you willing to commit to that? I cannot stress enough one important part: When you ask for consent, it must be a legitimate question. You cannot ask it and then still move forward if they answer no. If they do not genuinely consent to the conversation, then they are not a willing participant in it. If they do not genuinely accept and consent to the suggestions, changes, or accountabilities at the end of the conversation, then you are giving orders and should not be surprised if your teammate is disengaged.

Building on the conversation above about the incomplete assignment, after you've laid out the reason for the conversation, you might add: "I know that we set aside time for this conversation, and I want to make sure that you're okay to have it. Is this something you're ready for us to talk about?"

The end of this conversation, after you've come up with some proposed solutions together, could go something like this:

You: "Thanks again for having this conversation today. To recap, we talked about [insert various solutions here]. Did I miss anything or does that cover everything we'd talked about?"

Them: "No, that's everything."

You: "Great. Do these all seem like reasonable solutions to you? Are you comfortable with everything we came up with?"

Them: "Yes, that all works for me." (This is an ideal response. But if something doesn't work for them, you'll have to do more to arrive at a solution you both agree on.)

Authentic consent is an agreement between two parties so that no one feels pressured or taken advantage of.

It's a sign of respect, and making it a requirement creates an environment of safety. It belongs in every part of life.

"Apologize Immediately" by Chris Brogan

Author, journalist, and marketing consultant Chris Brogan wrote a blog post called "Apologize Immediately." In this article, Chris shares "the rule of Three A's," which he describes as "a great way to improve your relationships, at work, at home, and wherever you interact with humans."

"The Three A's" is a useful framework for leadership and customer service, and even in your personal and romantic relationships. They are:

1 Acknowledge
2 Apologize
3 Act

This represents a sequential order for conversations, where you first acknowledge (or validate) what the other person says, whether they voice a complaint, frustration, a feeling, or anything else. After that, you sincerely apologize. Don't use corporate-speak. Use empathy. Whatever you acknowledge should be something you care enough about to apologize for. The final step is to act—you tell them what you will do about the situation. Hopefully, your answer is not: do nothing.

I have used this framework for years, and it's magical. It has turned people who are upset into people who feel heard and cared for—for example, when I had to calm down a client who didn't like some design work our team had done:

> You're right, this design work is not up to the standard that you expect from us. We're sorry that this didn't hit the mark. I know this is an important project for you and you were planning to launch next week. I'm going to regroup with our design team, move some things around, and come back with some new designs for you to review by end of day tomorrow.

You can also use this strategy proactively, even before someone is outwardly upset, as I do when I've talked over people.

> Hey, I know there have been a few times recently when I've interrupted you or talked over you in meetings. I'm really sorry about that. It's not my intention to imply that your contributions aren't important or to steal your spotlight. Over the course of the next few meetings, I'm going to put myself on mute and make sure not to chime in until you've finished what you're saying.

After validating, apologizing, and then describing the action you will be taking, you may want to add one more step: Ask. You can ask a question either to gain consent for the action or to gather additional information that will help you deliver on that action.

The Ask step gives the other person the opportunity to agree with your proposed action or offer an alternative. If their alternative doesn't work, you can go back through the three A's. Continue to repeat this until a solution is found. This might sound like a lot of work, but in my experience, it is worth it. People who have been acknowledged, apologized to, and offered a resolution through action tend to soften substantially and become more reasonable and understanding.

Honesty and Transparency

This may sound obvious, but if you want to build trust, you must be trustworthy. If you are discovered hiding something or, worse, lying, it can take a long time to earn back that trust. In order for you to be trusted, people must sense that you are not hiding information from them; therefore, transparency and honesty are critical.

As stated earlier, consistency sets the stage for trust to be built. If trust is the degree to which you believe that your expectations will be met, then lies, deception, and deliberately hiding information are all inherently disruptive to trust. Each subverts or confuses the expectation of consistency. Let me illustrate this.

Say you're married, and every day for the last three years, you've woken up and made your partner breakfast. You go downstairs, brew coffee, prepare a breakfast sandwich with cage-free eggs, artisanal ham, and a nice aged cheddar. You even toast the bread. You drive your partner to work, kiss them goodbye, and drive off. It's your morning routine. You love it, and you're used to it. After work, you get in the car and pick up your partner in front of their office. Then one of you says to the other, "So, what do you want to do for dinner?"

One day, you arrive to pick up your partner from work and you see them lip-locked with someone else. Betrayal! *J'accuse!*

You wonder how long it's been going on. How serious is it? What else don't you know?

It's a story as old as time itself, but this classic tale of infidelity is the most obvious example of how a lie shakes your truth.

There's no question that someone reading this book right now has been through something like this story above, and my guess is that someone reading this has also been lied to at work.

I was once told by a business partner that I was "a valuable partner," while behind my back, he was looking for ways to get rid of me. I've witnessed managers looking employees squarely in the eyes and telling them everything is fine, while at the same time they're drawing up the paperwork to lay them off—during the holidays.

What do all the lies, white lies, and half-truths have in common? They all render words meaningless. If your people cannot trust the words coming out of your mouth, then how are you going to rally them behind you when you really need them? Right now, consciously or unconsciously, too many businesses rely on the fact that people are trapped because of their paycheck or health insurance.

That's not leadership. If you care for your people and understand the importance of trust, then you know that another aspect of love is the willingness to be honest, even when it requires vulnerability. By being honest and transparent, you offer your people the bare minimum of respect—the respect of giving them enough information to make informed decisions. By hiding information, you're manipulating them.

I understand that honesty is not always easy. Even more, I know that transparency is not always easy. But both are always right. If you have to lie or obfuscate information, then maybe what you're doing isn't all that right. And while I'm sure someone reading this is going on about "need to know" information, I'll just quote what Mike Monteiro said in his book, *Ruined by Design*: "I'm sure there are exceptions to this rule, *but they are exceptions*" (emphasis mine).

In the vast majority of circumstances, you can bring honesty and transparency into your leadership role without any long-term negative consequences. You may have to deal with some discomfort. For that, I'm sorry, but it comes with the job sometimes. At least you'll always have your integrity, and your people will appreciate that you respect them.

Ownership, Accountability, and Leading by Example

If you want to be trusted by your team, then you need to understand the concept of *ownership*. Ownership is a mindset. It requires that you hold yourself singularly responsible for the outcome of a situation. When you operate from a sense of ownership, you commit to placing yourself in service of the goal while putting blame and ego off to the side. Ownership requires you to

- make sacrifices
- be accountable for failure
- work harder

Witnessing someone who lifts accountability to the level of ownership is inspiring. When you can model this mindset for your team and encourage them to relate to their work in the same way, you create the conditions for a team that will succeed.

The phrases "that's not my job" and "it wasn't my fault" do not exist in cultures of ownership. In fact, the way leaders relate to fault and praise in ownership cultures is distinctly different from standard teams:

- If their teammates fail at something, leaders who take ownership assume the blame and commit to being better prepared next time.

- If their teammates succeed at something, leaders who take ownership revel in their teammates' growth and do not take credit for the success.

If you take credit for another's accomplishment, then others may do the same, and what will that do to your team culture? If you take responsibility for someone else's failure and commit to helping them avoid it in the future, then others may do the same, and what will *that* do to your team culture? It shouldn't be hard to envision how much more effective a team of owners is than a team of individuals concerned with protecting themselves by avoiding blame.

You must model the behavior you want your team to exhibit. Your behavior sets the standard for what is acceptable. As I've been saying all along, leadership is not about your ego, but about results—*our* results, not *your* results. It's also about growing your people into the best they can be.

Are you ready to indulge another Superhero story as an example?

Toward the end of *Avengers: Age of Ultron*, the blockbuster sequel to the first Avengers movie, Clint Barton, known as "Hawkeye," leads by example and, in doing so, changes the entire course of the Marvel Cinematic Universe (MCU).

The entire city of Sokovia is being thrust into the air by the villain robot known as Ultron, whose evil plan is to drop the city from the upper atmosphere to cause an extinction-level event for humanity. All of the Avengers are attempting to stop Ultron from executing his plan.

In a pivotal moment, Hawkeye must convince Wanda Maximoff to join him and fight. Wanda, known as "Scarlet Witch," is one of the most powerful characters in the entire MCU, but she is terrified. In the face of extraordinary danger, Clint (and not without nodding to the audience about the ridiculousness of the situation) shows us how to lead. As an epic battle rages beyond the walls of the building they are temporarily sheltered in, Clint demands to know if Wanda is up for the fight. She stares at him, frozen with fear, as he declares he will go back out and fight, with only his bows and arrows, and if she fights too, she will be an Avenger. He draws his bow and steps out the door.

Clint Barton doesn't have any supernatural abilities. He can't fly. He doesn't have superpowered strength or healing. He's just very accurate with his weapon.

By contrast, Scarlet Witch has an abundance of abilities, including telekinesis, flight, force-field generation, telepathy, and reality manipulation. She is powerful beyond measure... but she is scared. When she sees Clint walk out that door, something in her changes, and she goes on to become a central character in that moment and in future movies.

You may have someone on your team who is tremendously more "powerful" than you are, but maybe they don't know it yet. Maybe they are scared. The heroes on your team need your leadership as an example that inspires them to take ownership.

Tip: Have integrity and own the moral high ground. As a leader, everything you do is a verse in the story of you. Your ongoing, daily demeanor has a profound impact. Think of every action and decision as a domino that triggers an entire universe of events in the future. Consider that the way you treat others and how you behave now will be the legacy you leave behind:

- If you lie and you are found out, you become a liar.

- If you raise your voice to your team and scold them, you are aggressive.

- If you take all of the credit for your team's success, you're unappreciative and egotistical.

- If you make unethical decisions, you are an unethical person.

- If you do not create an environment of safety and inclusion, you will lose the opportunity to build the best team, hire the best talent, and accomplish your highest potential.

You have no idea who your team members will meet with or know in the future, or what organization they might move on to next. The people you have wronged in the past may be the same ones speaking to your candidate of the present and thereby impacting your success in the future.

So, ask yourself, if you came back from the future, what choices would you undo? What decisions would you change?

You are not perfect. I am not perfect. There is no perfect leader. You are not striving for perfection, either. You are striving for integrity, which will follow you everywhere you go. You will make mistakes as a leader, but you are both the sum and the average of your actions. People will be quicker to forgive and move forward if they trust your intentions.

Take out the trash sometimes

Wil Reynolds, the founder of Seer Interactive, a Philadelphia-based SEO agency, talks about taking out the trash. His point is about stepping in where necessary, even as the CEO, whether that means answering the phone or taking out the garbage. He even went so far as to mention it when he did a CEO swap with Rand Fishkin of Moz.

Whereas a "boss" will make sure to let you know what is technically "your job," great leaders step in when they are needed. It should naturally feel less important to stay rigid to what's technically your job when your mindset is about sacrificing so your team can win. As a lovable leader, you will do whatever is necessary to help your team succeed.

Doing this shows your team you are one of them. They need to know that you understand them, that you know what it's like, and that you are not above doing what needs to be done to support the team. That said, as the leader, you also need to know when to call it quits (as Fishkin rebutted when his CEO swap with Reynolds ended).

The point is not that you must take out the garbage or do the work for your team. It's that you need to be *willing* to step in and lend a hand when you're needed.

LOVABLE LEADER'S CHEAT SHEET

To build trust, I will:

- Sit on the same side of the table by

  - setting the table (conversation context, stating and aligning goals),
  - listening,
  - practicing curiosity,
  - validating (instead of judging),
  - aligning, and
  - getting consent.

- Remember the Three A's: Acknowledge, Apologize, Act. Plus, Announce and Ask.

- Be honest and transparent.

- Be consistent.

- Take full ownership (but not credit or blame) for my team's success or failure.

SAFE TRAVELS

Whenever you plan a vacation, you automatically assume you'll arrive at your destination safely. You put faith in the pilot's readiness to do their job and in their ability to fly the plane. You expect the floatation devices and oxygen masks will work in the event of an emergency. In business, you've got to create conditions in which your team members, too, feel safe in your hands as you lead them.

LOVABLE LEADERS start with care and trust—people-focused qualities that require emotional labor. With just care and trust, you've got the conditions for a great team, but you haven't led anyone anywhere yet.

To be a leader, you need to be going somewhere, which is why the third element of lovable leadership is about traveling. All travel requires two things: a destination and a reliable method of getting there. Leaders must focus on:

- **Goals:** You must set goals, but it's imperative that you get there safely.

- **Safety:** You must create safety for your teams, but to be a leader, you need to be going somewhere.

Safe travels include defining your team, setting goals, embracing conflict, and repairing.

Who Should Be on Your Team?

At the start of your journey, you'll want to make sure you have the right team in place. This is the stage at which you must explicitly state the values of your team, and the vision. By focusing on these attributes first and connecting with something deeper than a person's résumé, you increase the likelihood that all of your team members will be willing to work together toward the same goal.

This exercise can immediately, unintentionally go off track, because we tend to hire people who are just like us. You see this in start-up culture all the time: a brilliant twenty-something white guy partners with his close friends—all who happen to be white guys in their twenties—and launches a company. It's not long before the boys' club is back in business, and the environment is challenging for women and BIPOC (Black, Indigenous, and people of color) members.

There are benefits to a homogeneous team. For instance, when everyone shares a similar background, cultural references are understood, jokes are inoffensive, and work can often move quickly. However, this leads to glaring blind spots both strategically and culturally. This is why the definition of a team should point to something deeper. There are certain commitments of a lovable team. If you can build your team vision and values while honoring these principles, you should be on the right path toward building a dynamic, diverse, inclusive, and safe team where everyone can show up as their best selves.

These are the eight commitments of a team that can travel together safely:

1 Safety and protection
2 Communication guidelines
3 Alignment
4 Ownership
5 Growth
6 Courage
7 Resilience
8 Cooperation

Let's look at each of these in more detail.

1. Safety and protection
As the leader you must set a shining example, but every member of the team must embrace the call to safety. Each person must commit to stepping up and protecting their teammates. You must create an environment in which, if a team member feels disrespected, discriminated against, on the receiving end of microaggressions,

or unsafe because of harassment of any kind, they trust, without *any* fear of repercussions, that those concerns will be addressed seriously. Likewise, if a team member sees something inappropriate, it is their duty to speak up. Bad behavior that is overlooked is implicitly endorsed.

No one, no matter how valuable, how high on the org chart, or how long their tenure is, can be exempt from accountability for their actions. This is not to say that all incidents must end with dismissal from the team. However, people being held accountable should never expect retribution, only reconciliation and commitment to resolving the issues.

This commitment to safety and protection is an ongoing learning experience for everyone on the team because we all bring our bad habits and unconscious biases with us. None of us know what we don't know. Accepting this, we work on it. We commit to it.

A substantial part of creating an environment of safety and a culture of protection is a commitment to fight discrimination in all of its forms, and to create a culture of equity by focusing on diversity, inclusion, and representation.

Admittedly, diversity and inclusion is not my area of expertise, so I will be brief. But I believe it is extremely important for all leaders to educate themselves. I have included books on diversity and inclusion in the Additional Reading section at the end of this book. They are good places to start to learn more about this subject.

Every team member must commit to fighting prejudice and discrimination on behalf of their team. No matter who you are, how you were raised, or what you look like—but especially if you are a cisgender, straight, white male reading this book—you are responsible for creating a safe environment for *all* of your team members in which to grow.

Representation at all levels of the company is crucial for creating an environment where people are safe and included. It's not enough to hire diverse people so that you can put them on your website and check the diversity box.

According to the *Harvard Business Review* article "Diversity Doesn't Stick without Inclusion" by Laura Sherbin and Ripa Rashid, inclusive leadership "is a conglomeration of six behaviors: ensuring that team members speak up and are heard; making it safe to propose novel ideas; empowering team members to make decisions; taking advice and implementing feedback; giving actionable feedback; and sharing credit for team success."

Your responsibility is to ensure not only that you build a diverse team but also that you include each person on that team. Opportunities for advancement need to be thoughtfully put together with the help of varying viewpoints. Opportunities for advancement must also be communicated in a way that does not allow the language and framing of the position to exclude applicants of varying races, abilities, genders, and sexual orientations or gender identities from pursuing them.

None of this should sound groundbreaking, right? Yet, despite the commonsensical nature of creating a safe environment with equal opportunity, many companies simply do not. Whether because of unconscious bias or flat-out discrimination, many teams struggle to implement diversity programs and the subsequent inclusion.

Discrimination and bias can show up in policies around dress codes or conduct that may unfairly disadvantage minorities, women, or members of the LGBTQIA+ community. Some of these policies position a certain way of dressing or certain hairstyles as "unprofessional." They may not consider how those policies reinforce a discriminatory position that punishes one culture for not assimilating into the dominant or in-group culture.

For years, the conversation around culture has been about finding people who fit. When you find people who fit, you're filling open space. Often, the people who most easily fit that open space are the same as those already there. A better approach is to focus on *adding* to your culture. To avoid creating an exclusive and homogenous culture, look for people who bring new perspectives, different backgrounds, and unique personalities.

The best web developer for your team is not necessarily local. The best strategist for your team didn't necessarily go to an ivy league school. The best CFO isn't necessarily a man. The best project manager isn't necessarily neurotypical. The best HR manager isn't necessarily cisgender.

If you are truly committed to putting together the best team, then it needs to be open to and safe for everyone.

2. Communication guidelines

Every team member must commit to understanding the impact of their words and actions, and agree to communication guidelines that create opportunities for understanding and growth. This commitment sets the expectations for everyone about how communication will be handled. Everyone should be on the same page about how they will speak to others and how they can expect to be spoken to.

Note: This is not about tone policing. If someone has been harmed through harassment or discrimination, the communication guidelines do not apply to the person who has been harmed. This commitment is about everyday communication.

For example, Karen commits a racist microaggression against Barbara. It is not Barbara's responsibility to "be nice" and frame her feedback in a way that doesn't make Karen feel "uncomfortable." It is Karen's responsibility to take accountability and make amends.

If Donald makes a sexually suggestive remark to Cindy, she does not have to "calm down and be more respectful"—her emotional response to the harm is not the issue, his harmful actions are.

All teams, whether they be sports, business, military, or anything else, will have different communication expectations. There will be varying degrees of comfort as it relates to speed, directness, and tone.

In general, I believe that the most effective communication is

- direct
- concise
- honest
- thoughtful
- respectful

This is an ideal combination for a variety of reasons. When communication is *direct*, there is no need to try to interpret meaning. When it is *concise*, there is less chance of getting lost amid unnecessary details. When it is *honest*, there is never a need to second-guess the intentions. When it is *thoughtful*, people communicate after they've considered what they are saying, why they are saying it, and what they hope to accomplish by saying it. When it is *respectful*, people are less likely to take the information as a personal attack and leap to defend themselves.

Kindness can be added to the list. When your communication is kind, you will naturally refrain from making underhanded or passive-aggressive comments. I know some organizations thrive on brutal honesty, but I've yet to find someone who takes issue with kindness.

Tip: Be aware of "The Rift." The easiest way to cause a rift between you and someone else is with words. Everyone on your team must understand this. Sometimes it's careless, sometimes thoughtless. The tone of what is said could be intentional or unintentional... It doesn't matter, because it is not forgotten. We may forgive, but we do not forget those who hurt us or the sting of those words. When we are hurt, we trust a little less and protect ourselves more.

Poor communication is a liability. Too often, we say things in the heat of the moment only to realize later on that we were wrong, had bad information, or would have accomplished a better result with different words and tone. This is why I stress to my clients, my team, and my friends the importance of carefully considering words and tone. While the rift can also be mended with words, it will take much longer to repair than it did to create it.

As a lovable leader, you must be clear in your vision so, as a result, you walk softly, gather all of the information, and give thoughtful responses designed to produce the most positive outcome. You see little benefit in accusations or causing people to feel bad, as it is rarely the way to build loyalty or inspire hard work.

Be careful with your words, knowing that once something has been spoken, it cannot be taken back. Negativity can be infectious. When a true outbreak occurs, it can spread rapidly to infect even the most optimistic team members. The consequences of spreading negativity can be dire.

The best organizations don't take sides against each other internally... they are all on the same side. By equipping your team with the tools for respectful and productive conversations, you create an environment in which everyone feels comfortable dealing with problematic situations directly.

3. Alignment

Great teams succeed not because of their individual talents but because of their willingness to align around a mission together. On a high-functioning team, accountability for team alignment is held by the group. This must be a shared responsibility. Each team member needs to be willing to align with the team and keep their teammates moving in the same direction too. As the old adage goes, "a chain is only as strong as its weakest link."

A great team will be committed not just to the destination but also to the process of getting there.

Note, however, that alignment is different from agreement. Alignment often requires people to disagree and still solve problems in the service of moving together toward something bigger.

4. Ownership

Every team member must commit to taking complete ownership of their role and team. As I mentioned earlier, leaders take ownership. If you want a team of leaders, then you need a team of owners.

Owners step up even when it's not their responsibility. Owners acknowledge their mistakes and failures and take it upon themselves to fix the problem. Accountability and ownership are contagious. You don't want to be in a babysitter role, assigning blame and trying to get people to take their jobs seriously. You want people committed to ownership from day one.

5. Growth

If you try to change how people do their jobs, the results are likely to be shallow and short-lived. If someone truly commits to building a new habit and sees their efforts rewarded, you may see success. But when you merely teach someone what to do, they will not be well equipped to adapt. To succeed in both structured and instructed situations, you need to change how they think.

One of my clients (let's call her Ava), was a new manager for a coworking space. She was responsible for training a new junior associate on giving tours and selling the space to prospective tenants. The associate, Michelle, was young and relatively inexperienced in sales. Like many people, she didn't really like sales. She said it felt "icky." Because it was Ava's job to help her junior associate develop her sales competency, naturally, she began by testing Michelle on raw information:

- What different sizes are the office spaces?
- Can members get their mail delivered here?
- What sorts of companies work in this space?
- Where is the coffee?

I reminded Ava that all these questions could be answered on a sheet of paper or listed on a website. Obviously, it was important that Michelle knew the answers. However, memorization of the facts would not help her become a better salesperson, but simply a more animated FAQ page.

What could Ava do? Would handing Michelle a script help? What about reviewing the steps of the process? How about providing the most effective sales tools or commonly requested resources?

Although all those things would assist Michelle and make the job a little "easier" and more "comfortable," they wouldn't turn her into a better salesperson because they wouldn't change her relationship to the act of selling. But that's what Ava was after. How could Ava transform Michelle into a sales rock star? When it's a question of growth, the answer usually isn't in providing more information; it's in the mindset.

Ava loves sales, and she is phenomenal at it. So, I asked her to think about the way she sold, to analyze what she would think about during a sales appointment, and to explore the feeling of exhilaration she gets as a sale is about to close.

After some digging into her own psyche, Ava realized that when she met someone in a sales appointment, she was excited because that person could be the newest addition to *her* community. Because it was *her* community, she felt complete ownership and pride, and she was fiercely protective. When she played out the whole thought process, she realized that, ultimately, she was on a mission to create a space where everyone loves coming into work.

For Ava, this vision drove every sale. This gave her confidence and motivation in sales situations. It allowed her to be friendly and calm. It's what made sales so easy for her.

Great! So, now we knew how we wanted her associate to feel. There was just one problem: she couldn't give Michelle that motivation, confidence, or calm and friendly demeanor like a Hallmark card. She had to plant the seed that would grow into that mindset. In this example, that seed is ownership. So, Ava set out to plant the seed for a new mindset and then proceeded to water it until it blossomed.

She started by talking to Michelle regularly about the ownership mindset. She spoke to her as an equal and a peer rather than as a manager. Ava gave Michelle freedom while still making herself available to support her. She introduced Michelle to every existing tenant and encouraged her to get to know them so that she, too, felt like part of the community. Once Michelle began thinking like an owner, she was no longer selling. She was building and protecting something that belonged, in part, to her.

Leadership often can be as simple as illuminating something that someone else would not have seen without the light you shine.

6. Courage

Every team member must commit to bold and courageous acts for the team. Great leaders are willing to venture into the unknown and take risks. They present calmness and clarity in the face of adversity. They thrive under pressure. These are the people who always rise to the occasion.

Now, imagine an entire team of people like this.

Alexander the Great said, "I am not afraid of an army of lions led by a sheep; I am afraid of an army of sheep led by a lion." Can you imagine what Alexander might have thought about an army of lions led by a lion? A courageous team will continuously push forward with a dauntless leader out front forging the way.

7. Resilience

To deal with problems, you must embrace the principle of resilience. How you build and lead your team must encourage and foster resilience.

Problems will arise even upon mastery of the lovable leader concept. (I know, I was shocked too.) No organization is perfect. Team members won't always agree. Work won't always be up to your standards. But business and leadership aren't about perfection, and in some ways they aren't even about the pursuit of perfection. Instead, pursue an ever-improving ability to navigate complex situations and rectify mistakes.

Leadership is about being resilient in the face of adversity and challenges. Team members may fight, even in the best organizations. Projects will run long, miss deadlines, and go over budget. And—I hate to break it to you—there will be difficult conversations with your team. Sorry, but it's the truth.

That said, there are ways to deal with conflict effectively, and ways to make the situation worse. Before you can even approach conflict resolution, you must first set the conditions on your team that properly contextualize conflict as an expected part of the process.

In a lovable leadership environment, people should feel supported and, as a result, comfortable addressing problems directly, productively, and in a tone that yields positive outcomes. If team members don't feel as though they can be honest and forthright, then the conditions for productive conversations have been suppressed by a lack of trust. People must feel comfortable enough to have open and honest discussions and be equipped with the tools to ensure that those conversations yield productive outcomes.

These are the conditions for a resilient organization. When conflict is seen as a standard component of any organization, it can be reframed as a tool to make your team stronger by way of how you overcome adversity.

Think of conflict as similar to Kintsugi. Kintsugi (meaning "golden repair") is the Japanese art of repairing

broken pottery with lacquer dusted or mixed with pow-
dered gold, silver, or platinum, a method similar to the
Japanese maki-e technique. As a philosophy, Kintsugi
treats breakage and repair as part of the history of an
object rather than as something to disguise.

Our cracks, scratches, and scars are the very things
that make us stronger as people. The unchallenged individual is rarely the strongest, and the person who has
seen only modest adversity is ill-equipped to handle it
in the future. Great teams triumph in spite of adversity.
Team members may fight with one another along the
way, but once they overcome their differences and bond
together, they are far stronger than they ever could've
been without the struggle.

8. Cooperation

My wife has a group of friends from college with whom
we get together twice a year. We play a lot of board games
and the occasional game of beer pong. One game we routinely play is called You Don't Know Jack Trivia Murder
Party. It's a series of fun trivia games with a humorous
horror movie theme. It's a terrific party game. In it, a
small challenge called "Decisions, Decisions" adapts the
classic Prisoner's Dilemma.

In this game, there is a pile of money. You can choose
to take it or not. If nobody takes the money, nobody dies.
If some take the money, everyone who didn't will die. If
you all take the money, all of you die. Players who take
the money will earn $2,000 divided by the number of
players who took the money.

Only one move here is mutually beneficial. If we cooperate and no one takes the money, then everyone makes it out alive. But no matter how many times I've played this game with this group, no one has ever taken me up on the offer to leave the money, and inevitably, I die.

The incentive in this game is to win, and therefore, most people feel the smartest move is to screw over the competition. In a party video game, that is the smartest move, and given my track record, I *should* probably start taking the money. However, in your career, the smartest option is often to survive another day and live to fight another battle. The goal shouldn't be for *me* to win; it should be for *us* to win. Life, unlike trivia games, does not have to be a zero-sum game.

It's easy to see why we fall for it. Life can often *feel* like a game of "me against the world." Many of us have worked in jobs where we had to prove ourselves, justify our time or actions, or fight for the right to be heard or respected. Hands up if you've ever felt that way.

But when we see life with a "me against the world" mindset, someone always wins and someone always loses. Someone must be right. Someone must be wrong. Applying this mindset to your leadership is a dicey game. You see team members as subordinates, and your conversations go a particular way. You reactively let everyone know what they have done wrong and what they must improve to regain your favor. But when you attack, naturally, they defend. Except, unlike in trivia games, everyone loses.

Consider that as you detail every reason your team member is wrong, they might be doing something else:

- Protecting their ego by rationalizing with excuses.

- Finding logical reasons they are not wrong.

- Seeking out someone else to divert the blame to.

- Searching their mental database for every instance you've not done what you said what you would.

Hooray for progress, right?

A FEW months later, every interaction that same employee has with you is tainted by preconceived ideas about how you will behave. Based on your previous attack, they come ready to defend. How will it impact your work environment when people are walking around with their defenses up?

The only way to win in this real-life game is to change the rules. What if instead of playing against each other in a game of "attack and defend," you could play "join teams together"?

This calls into question what it means to win. Many people approach conflict seeking to overpower others with their ideas and perspectives and so achieve victory, but the lovable leader takes a different approach. A lovable leader's version of a win is when both parties walk away with more trust in each other, rather than less. A lovable leader wins when both parties feel heard and acknowledged. Winning in the context of lovable leadership is a win-win situation, not a win-lose situation. And when you exemplify this cooperative approach as well as expect it from the rest of your team toward each other, you are fostering an environment that is conducive to success in the pursuit of common goals.

Goals, Productive Conflict, and Repairs

Chapter 7 is all about setting goals, so regarding goals and safe travels, I'll be brief and simply say that, if you have care and trust, and you've assembled the best team of members who have all made the eight commitments, you still need somewhere to go—that is, toward your goals. They are the part that technically makes you a leader. The other qualities are what make you worth following.

Along the way toward any destination, problems are likely. These problems can be minor, like a miscommunication, a disagreement over something small, or a goal not being hit on time. They can also be about something major and consequential such as two teammates refusing to work together, a fundamental disagreement about the end goals, or a complete breakdown in operations that threatens the entire mission.

Regardless of the situation, action is almost universally preferable to inaction, even if action will create conflict. In fact, conflict is one of your most important tools.

"Productive conflict" is a term I've been using for years, but you may be more familiar with it from Liane Davey's book *The Good Fight*. Regardless of whether your introduction to the topics is here, through *The Good Fight*, or somewhere else, here's the gist of it: people tend to avoid conflict and have negative associations with the word. I see conflict as a resoundingly positive event.

Conflict is a collision between two things. The outcome of a conflict is a resolution. Therefore, deliberately engaging in conflict is the fastest path to a resolution.

In situations where you are at an impasse of indecision or waiting on something to happen, you can initiate conflict to arrive at the next step.

For example, say you're a videographer and you're waiting on your client to give you feedback on the first draft so that you can finish the project before your next one starts. The client is already two days late. If you don't get the feedback in the next forty-eight hours, the entire timeline will be thrown off. As a result, you will have to either postpone the project for a full month, which will push back your upcoming project, or work nights and weekends to get it all done. Any of these options could be costly. What should you do?

Many people would quietly stew and be upset. Perhaps they'd even let this anxiety or frustration cause them to lash out at the client or take a tone that conveys impatience. But you're a lovable leader, and you know that the better move is to initiate productive conflict. Sure, you could send an email, but you know it could take a day or more for them to even see it. So, you call them. Your goal for the call is to use the conflict in order to resolve what will definitively happen next. You say:

> Hi John, I wanted to give you a quick call. I know you're busy, but I also know how important this project is to you. I'm currently awaiting feedback from your team, and I wanted to give you the heads-up. I have another project starting in ten days, and I want to

make sure I can deliver your project in time. If I get the feedback from you in the next forty-eight hours, I'll still have time to deliver your project. If not, I'm going to have to postpone the final deliverable for about a month. How would you like to proceed? Shall we push the project back, or do you think your team will have the feedback in time?

There is close to a zero percent chance that you end that phone call without a resolution.

Productive conflict is a method by which you can initiate a collision in the service of resolving inaction or uncertainty. When you experience a problem with another team member, addressing it as soon as possible and directly allows for discussion and resolution instead of letting negative emotions fester in your or their mind. In situations where any sort of decision needs to be made, creating a space for the collision of options facilitates an outcome.

These sorts of conflicts are the key to team alignment, transparency, and trust. Practice the eight commitments to ensure that your conflicts are productive rather than destructive. Even conflict must feel like a safe space in which to communicate and work through problems and ideas.

The final component of safe travels is about repairs— fixing things when they break. In chapter 9, I cover various conflict resolution scenarios and provide a full toolkit for managing problems. What's important regarding safe travels is your ongoing commitment to fixing things as they break. Sometimes, you will have to replace a team member. Sometimes, you will have to revisit your goals and strategy. You need to maintain a mindset of accepting and embracing change and being willing to do the work to make repairs.

But What About Fear?

It's true that it is easier to become a feared leader than it is to become loved. But is it more effective? This is a rhetorical question. And there is no one distinct answer to it. Humans are too complex and differing for one rule of behavior to fit all. So, I'd be foolish to suggest that *every* great leader was lovable. But I don't think it's outlandish to claim that few of history's most effective leaders caused their teams to operate in perpetual states of fear.

The stress of regularly feeling fear can lead to serious physical and emotional problems that can reduce people's effectiveness and productivity. When we are scared, we operate in self-preservation mode to survive. Certainly, in certain scenarios and when applied properly, fear can be a useful tool, but it also causes infighting and backstabbing. When overused or used at the wrong time, fear can destroy productivity and morale and even permanently decimate a relationship.

Fear-based leaders may suggest that the fear keeps their team focused and compliant, and that love-based leadership is wimpy and commands no respect or power. Love-based leaders may believe that their approach keeps teams happy and motivated, and that tyrannical leadership alienates good employees, who will leave the moment something better comes around.

To either perspective, I would say that the world is not so black and white. Somewhere between fear and love, there must be examples of leaders who command a healthy respect, based in fear, in an otherwise loving environment. Creating an environment in which you are trusted and where fear is replaced with respect is possible.

In truth, it doesn't take much to make this shift. If your leadership comes with a title or implied authority, don't lean on it. There is no need—your authority is understood. You will command far more respect and have far more success with a simple shift. Pivot from sitting across the table, where you lean on the fear response that arises when people fear losing their job, to sitting on the same side of the table, where you can put the focus back on shared goals and your willingness to offer support. Don't use threats to coerce action. Speak of support, instead, such that the consequences of failure would be shared by both of you.

For example, instead of, "Joe, you need to start hitting quota. I'm putting you on a thirty-day performance plan. If you don't start making significant progress, we're going to need to go in a different direction," a lovable leader would say: "Joe, more than anything, I want to see you succeed in this role. Right now I know you're struggling, but I want to help. Let's talk about what sort of support you need from me and the team so you have what you need to start consistently hitting your quotas. I want you to continue being a part of this team, so let's figure out how we can make that happen."

We feel the need to announce our authority to exact punishment and harm only when our egos feel threatened or we have chosen not to use our influence and kindness. Be thoughtful about your role. Do not cause your team to worry constantly and panic whenever something goes wrong. Lovable leaders wield not only influence but also respect. This is how teams with intense loyalty and grit are built.

LOVABLE LEADER'S CHEAT SHEET

Safe travels means I will:

- Make sure it is safe on the way toward our goals.

- Guide the team to make commitments that ensure safety, because our team is defined by what we commit to.

- Ensure we all embrace productive conflict to resolve uncertainty or inaction.

- Be vigilant about making repairs to the team.

- Always choose to lead with love over fear.

YOUR MOST
IMPORTANT TOOL

*When it comes down to it, the only tools a leader
has are words, ideas, and actions. Therefore,
communication is your single most important tool as
a leader. Mastering the skill of communication is a lifelong
endeavor for the lovable leader to continually pursue.*

The Functions of Communication

Your communication determines your team's capacity for
success. As the graphic below illustrates, there are three
essential functions of communication—to inform, to
influence, and to inspire. Your capacity with these three
functions exists on a spectrum that begin with misin-
formation, incapacitation, and demotivation respectively.
When you master the art of communication to inform,
influence, and inspire, you will be more effective, create

environments for collaboration, and readily move every-one in the same direction.

SPECTRUM OF COMMUNICATION

Misinform/Confuse	Inform
Subordinate/Incapacitate	Influence
Demotivate	Inspire

Your success as a leader will depend on where your communication exists on these spectrums. So, let's briefly review all three functions before moving into an approach for mastering communication.

Inform

As a leader, your job is to ensure that your team has all the information they need to do their jobs effectively. However, you'll be effective at informing someone only if the message is received and accurately understood. This means that you need to understand how each member of your team best receives information.

Do they prefer an email so that they have a record to fall back on? Are they the type that prefers a five-minute face-to-face conversation? Do they need a quick white-board session to process the information visually? A simple way to know the answer is to just ask each person. Communicating in their preferred modes respects the various ways people process information. By adhering to their preferences, you also remove a potential excuse and place yourself in a better position if a team member is underperforming and you have to talk about it. More on this in chapter 9.

The second part of effectively delivering information is to make it clear. Being misunderstood wastes everyone's time. It is all too easy to believe that the email you just wrote is perfectly lucid, but reread it at least once, even out loud to yourself, to be doubly sure. Ensuring clarity in your communications is vital, but fostering an environment in which your team feels safe asking for clarification is even more important.

Influence

Despite what some may think, influence is not the same thing as manipulation. While both involve attempting to modify people's behaviors, manipulation is doing it solely for your own benefit and often using stress and coercion to remove people's ability to make choices in order to achieve those ends.

Influencing your team can range from light course correction to full-scale moving people from complete inaction to action. Ethically influencing your team requires that you

- do it for a common, aligned purpose

- be honest about your intentions and not resort to trickery or deception

- make sure the other person always has a choice

A lifelong commitment to learning the art of influence will help you in virtually every area of your life. In marketing and sales, you must persuade people of the value of your solution over a competing option. As a friend, you may find yourself rallying a group to pick a dinner restaurant or one person to help you move a couch into your apartment. As a leader, you often need to align multiple people with a single goal, are responsible for organizing and inspiring action, and may have tense conflicts to resolve. You are also responsible for ensuring that your team learns how to inspire action and resolve conflict. Learning how to influence people and modeling for your team how to be more influential in communication are both vital to your success.

To take a deep dive with this, I recommend reading both *Influence* and *Pre-Suasion* by Robert Cialdini.

Inspire

Shallow forms of inspiration take the form of motivational posters and quotes shared on social media platforms. Although these are easy to find, consume, and understand, they are ephemeral, at best. Powerful and long-lasting inspiration has to come from a deep desire to change something.

The secret to inspiration is quite simple:

- Find something that has profound meaning and importance to someone.

- Create a compelling and clear vision of how to accomplish or attain that something, ideally presented as a story.

- Be as committed as they are to seeing that vision come true by continually stoking the flames of excitement.

Imagine you're a start-up with a customer relations management (CRM) built for small businesses.

- You're not just trying to grow revenue by 25 percent this year. *You're on a mission to continually increase each team member's salary by helping 4,000 new small businesses grow this year with your easy-to-use CRM.*

- You're not going to "dig in and push harder this year than ever before." *You're a scrappy team, tightly bound together by a single idea: changing the lives of millions of small business owners. You work hard during the day and rest at night, so your clients can do the same thing. Your small business customers are your moms and dads, sisters and brothers, and hardworking people all across this country who need a partner that is working exclusively for them. That's you.*

- You're not just going to check the numbers and hold weekly accountability meetings to check the numbers. *You're supporting one another every day and ringing a giant cowbell every time a new business signs up for an annual plan. You're building a knowledge base to share best practices. You're reading customer stories at the weekly stand-up, making sure everyone remembers who you're working to help.*

Inspiration is active. It requires maintenance. There are far too many distractions in life to hold on to anything that doesn't carry deep significance. As a leader, your ability to inspire your team will determine their tenacity at work.

Communication can be your most effective tool. So be extremely thoughtful about it. The responsibility of your role requires you to be the most considerate about your choice of words and tone. You set the example of how the team communicates.

Communication Mastery

If you were to travel half the distance between two points over and over again, you would never reach your destination. Similarly, the pursuit of communications mastery is a journey that will last a lifetime. While you'll eventually become an extraordinary communicator if you pursue this path, you'll never be flawless, just consistently better and more effective.

Communication mastery is about increasing the likelihood that the intent of what you say is the same as what the recipient understands.

- If you intend to inform, did the person understand?
- If you intend to influence, was action taken?
- If you intend to inspire, did you inspire?

Furthermore, if your communication reflects you, is it an accurate reflection of who you have set out to be? Does your communication mirror your values? Is your communication helping you accomplish your personal goals and organizational goals?

Let's review some of the frameworks you'll need to become a master of communication.

Think in terms of signals

Everything you do is a signal to your team. Your reactions set their expectations about how you will react in the future. Your words today create a picture in their mind about what you will say tomorrow. Your actions alert them to your values and how you see your role on the team. Because everything is a signal:

- You don't gossip.

- You don't lose your temper.

- You are careful of how you talk to team members and clients.

- You are careful of how you treat people who are not on your team.

The example you set for your team shapes your culture. So get in the habit of examining your behavior and asking yourself: What am I signaling? Think about the type of culture you want to cultivate. Consider how you want people to talk to one another. Reflect on how you want people to relate to their role. Then, examine the signals you send to make sure your behaviors are conducive to your desired outcomes.

Pursue clarity

Honesty is essential to building trust, which is essential to clarity. As you know by now, the lovable leader model adheres to a strict code of honesty, without exception. Honest and kind communication is the model.

Clarity also involves being specific and comprehensive. As I touched on earlier, by being highly detailed in what you say and spending the time to ensure that what you've said was received as you intended it, you reduce the likelihood of errors or misunderstandings. If people trust what you are saying in the first place, they will take your words at face value rather than second-guessing the meaning behind them.

If you create an expectation of honesty and ensure complete understanding of your team members, you will have the conditions necessary to inspire people, manage conflict, create accountability, and accomplish your goals.

Holding others accountable for your own shortcomings in communication is unfair. If someone does not understand what you say or interpret what you say as you mean it, the communication breakdown is your mistake, not theirs. Ideally, they would take ownership. Ideally, they would ask follow-up questions so that they understand what you mean. Ideally, they would discuss it with you if trust needs to be repaired. However, none of that is under your control. You can control only how much ownership you take over the clarity of your communication.

If you send the right signals to your team, build the trust so that they can take you at face value, and then communicate clearly and explicitly, you will have created a culture in which people take ownership and accountability to pick up the slack in areas where you will inevitably fall short. But it is always your responsibility and burden to go the extra step to ensure you're clear.

A leader who leads by example, is trustworthy, and is both clear and kind is rare in this world. For anyone who has had even a few managers, you will stand out from the crowd if you do these things. It may sound like a lot of emotional labor, but once you build this habit, your relationships with your team will be stronger, you will deal with fewer misunderstandings, and you will breed the sort of loyalty that most managers can't even imagine.

LOVABLE LEADER'S CHEAT SHEET

To master the art of communication as a leader, I will:

- Remember the three functions of communication:

  - Inform,
  - Influence,
  - Inspire.

- Set an example for how the team communicates.

- Be cognizant of the signals my communication sends.

6

THE DESTINATION

*Author Deb Gabor likes to say, "If you aim at nothing,
you'll hit it with 100 percent accuracy every time."
As a leader, start with the target—in other words, know
the destination of your work. Understanding where
you want to go is critical because if you don't, you
are not leading... you are simply wandering.*

Purpose

Great leaders are almost never in it (solely or primarily) for the money. Money is actually a weak motivator. Studies have shown that employees are more likely to be moved by intrinsic motivators such as job satisfaction, feelings of belonging, and autonomy in their role than they are by extrinsic rewards such as bonuses. Although there are bound to be exceptions to the rule, most leaders are committed to something bigger than themselves, and to something more meaningful than money.

The longing to be a part of something bigger is baked into our human DNA. We are social creatures, many of us searching for our purpose in life. Great leaders answer that question and give their teams a defining mission and purpose. Great leaders show their team a vision for an ambitious future and align people with the values and work ethic required to make it a reality. This can be seen in mission statements but also in how work is framed on a day-to-day basis.

I'll give you an example

The Equitist is a company that helps "healthcare organizations move from health equity in theory, to action." At the bottom of their homepage (theequitist.co) they explain:

> We are at a pivotal juncture in society. Covid has been the most illustrative example of population health. It's clearly demonstrated that our health and wellness is connected to our neighbor's, that racism is still a pervasive poison that's killing our Black & Brown people at every turn, that our leaders are unprepared to execute on equity and paralyzed when it comes to challenging the status quo. Make no mistake about it. The stakes are high—it's now or never for embracing and actualizing health equity.

Led by Dr. Lauren R. Powell, president and CEO of The Equitist, this work is bigger than whatever profit the business earns. This is a business with purpose. The Equitist is out to do something for the world. Their work is less about them and more about their contribution.

By contrast, let's look at another example: "The Home Depot is in the home improvement business, and our goal is to provide the highest level of service, the broadest selection of products and the most competitive prices." Do you feel inspired?

Purpose inspires people to go beyond their believed limitations and think bigger. It awakens dreams and fuels immortality. And this is clearly something worth exploring, as "Gallup research shows that only 41% of U.S. employees strongly agree that they know what their company stands for and what makes it different from its competitors."

So, now that you have a grasp of purpose in action, let's talk about how to uncover purpose.

"Purpose" Is Not the Same Thing as "the Reason"

Why do we get up and go to work? It's a question I'm sure we've all asked ourselves. The obvious answer is that we exist in an economic system that requires work in exchange for money and money in exchange for the necessities of life. However, the reason we work becomes harder to pin down when we frame it in the context of "a life worth living." The logistical becomes existential.

In the midst of all the "woo-woo" company culture activities that so many organizations put themselves through, the word "purpose" gets thrown around a lot. While going through these check-the-box exercises, you don't have to listen too closely to realize that when many people think they are talking about purpose, they are really talking about the reason for doing something—which is simply the explanation of an action that considers and incorporates available data.

Purpose is rarely revealed during some standard fill-in-the-blank purpose-statement exercise in conference room D on Tuesday. Purpose is something deeper inside you.

Purpose as a Matter of Life and Death

After I got my driver's license in high school, my mother and I shared a car. On days when she didn't have errands to run, I would get the keys to her Jeep Grand Cherokee. On my last day of high school, we agreed that I would drive myself to school and meet her for lunch to give her the car. We were having a graduation party, and she wanted to go to the "good supermarket" one town over to get fish. Mom made a mean swordfish.

At a pizzeria, I got a slice and waited for my mom to arrive. Once she got there, I gave her the keys, and she dropped me off at school.

When I arrived home after school, I was met at the front door by my *bubbe* (Yiddish for grandmother). I could tell by her face that something was wrong. She explained to me that my mother had been in a car accident and was at the hospital. I learned that the trailer of a guaranteed-overnight-delivery truck had fishtailed and slammed into the driver's side of the Grand Cherokee.

Mom spent nine hours in the operating room. It took more than nine pints of blood to save her life. She was in a coma for the next three weeks. After she woke up, her recovery, though long and arduous, was remarkable... but she was never the same.

Before the accident, my mother had been attending Fordham University to get her master's degree in social work. She was on a scholarship from the American Association of University Women. That scholarship was given to only one person a year, and she had been selected among hundreds of applicants. She wanted to go into geriatric care, to help older adults and their families cope with aging and plan for end-of-life issues. After the accident, my mother had a hard time focusing, and her mood was erratic. She would go from smiling to screaming and shouting. All of these challenges meant that she wouldn't be able to continue the program. So, she never finished her degree or impacted people's lives the way she wanted to.

Sometimes I think if I'd ordered two slices, she might've avoided that accident. Before I left the pizza place, I considered going to the bathroom but decided to wait until I got back to school. Maybe if I had just gone to the bathroom, none of this would've happened.

I tell you this not because I blame myself for my mom's accident. I say it to impress upon you that it all happened in an instant. Her life and many other people's lives changed forever, and no one saw it coming.

Confront the reality of death with absolute clarity. Acknowledge that after you're gone, a world will remain. Now, consider how that realization should shape your day-to-day.

That is purpose. *That* sort of thinking is what I believe drives truly aspirational leaders. Think about your life in a context beyond the number of years you are alive to contribute to the story of our species.

What Will Your Verse Be?

You might think that I started a social media agency, True Voice Media, because I wanted to help companies use Twitter more effectively—but that barely scratches the surface of my true intentions. I did build social media strategies for organizations large and small. The purpose of those strategies, however, went well beyond immediate revenue implications.

You see, there is *what I did*, and then there is *why I did it*. I fundamentally believed that social media represented a collection of tools that reflected how companies operated. This included how they interacted with their customers, what their customers believed about the brand, and perhaps most importantly, how their employees represented the brand. Companies with great internal cultures produced employees who publicly advocated for their employer on social media, posting positive reviews. The employees would also mirror the company's culture in their public/social interactions with customers and prospects.

And so I often designed strategies that were less prescriptive of social media tactics and more illustrative of the internal changes necessary to build a culture that could capitalize on the inherently valuable properties of social media. I was helping companies understand why social media required them to work on themselves. The tactics truly only made sense in that context. The purpose of the work was to get companies to look at themselves and to take care of their employees, customers, and communities.

I repeated these messages about the vital importance of what social media tools and processes could enable. I said it over and over in team meetings and sales calls, and at networking functions. These messages conveyed the company's purpose, and each team member understood that this set us apart from the competition.

This purpose fueled our days. Our work was bigger than the money clients paid us and bigger than the tasks on our to-do list, and it provided more guidance than our Monday morning stand-up meetings. Furthermore, successfully advancing this purpose in the world implied organizational growth, opportunities for advancement, and the chance to be part of something extraordinary. So, aspects of this purpose also intrinsically and extrinsically motivated each team member.

We don't get up for work simply to ensure the company makes more money. That's not exciting on its own, and it's certainly not a purpose or reason to exist.

I like to recall a scene in the movie *Dead Poets Society*, in which John Keating (played by Robin Williams) talks about the beauty and passion of poetry as a metaphor for life. He quotes a poem by Walt Whitman:

O me! O life! of the questions of these recurring,

Of the endless trains of the faithless, of cities fill'd with the foolish,

...

What good amid these, O me, O life?

Answer.

That you are here—that life exists and identity,

That the powerful play goes on, and you may contribute a verse.

Keating asks the circle of rapt young students around him what their verses will be. Now ask yourself: What will your verse be? What is your driving purpose?

Aligning with "Something Bigger"

Once you've identified your purpose, ask yourself whether it will inspire your team members. Will they connect to it? Does it align with what they are out to accomplish in their lives?

It is not enough to ask your team to accomplish tasks that impact today or even tomorrow. Instead, each objective is a stepping stone to a larger and more ambitious purpose: to leave a lasting impact on the world or achieve a new level of accomplishment. Inspiring the belief in others that they are capable of something bigger, something that gives their life more meaning, is essential.

"Something bigger" will look different to everyone. Finding it requires you to understand the contribution your team members wish to make in the world.

Heroic example

At The Superhero Institute, I train and certify coaches in the Superhero methodology. These coaches then go on to train their clients to become Superheroes. The "something bigger" I gravitate toward in that, is the over-arching belief that the world would be better off with more people in it who are out to make a positive impact in the world by living The Superhero Code. (Remember that from the introduction?) For each of my coaches, however, there may be an individual aspect of the code that resonates with them the most within the overarching purpose. For example:

- A coach who grew up in traumatic or challenging circumstances may gravitate toward teaching the value of *resilience* from The Superhero Code.

- A coach who grew up with privilege may gravitate toward *self-sacrifice*.

- A coach who discovered themselves later in life by embracing discipline may find they align most with the code's call to *responsibility*.

While each of the coaches will gain new abilities that help them grow their revenues as a coach, that is nowhere to be found in the sales pitch for becoming a Superhero coach. Coaches who become certified through The Superhero Institute are invited to align behind something bigger.

What have you invited people to align themselves with?

If your purpose is only about changing the company's balance sheet, then you lack the conditions for lasting motivation. Finding another company that wants to make money is easy. So is job-hopping from one place to another in the pursuit of advancement in title and salary, if you're talented. How will you keep a valuable team member if all you have to offer is the same commodity as any other company: money? The answer is, you can't and you won't. You need something more. You need to think about how you will not only keep your best talent but also attract the best new talent. Many aspects of leadership described in this book will help with that. Among the most important is to find your North Star.

When people feel there is a purpose to their work, they will be intrinsically driven to work longer hours, put in more effort, and expend the mental energy into the realization of their objective.

Goals

Goals are a tangible marker for success. Leaders set goals to keep the team looking forward in pursuit of an objective in the distance.

There are several aspects of goal setting that you should keep in mind as a leader.

Be SMART

If you've ever played a sport, you know that there are certain conditions for when a point is officially scored and tallied. In basketball, the ball must go through the hoop. In football, it must cross the goal line. In baseball, the runner's foot must touch home plate. There are nuances to all of these, but you get the idea.

A goal, too, has conditions that need to be met in order to qualify. To know for certain that you've reached your goal, you must be able to definitively show whether it was completed.

This is why leaders should avoid setting vague goals. If it cannot be measured, you cannot determine whether it was accomplished. You've got to be able to objectively measure goals, rather than just subjectively feel they're done. This is why I encourage you to opt for goals that are SMART—that is, specific, measurable, attainable, relevant, and timely:

- A **specific** goal is a clearly defined outcome. Everyone involved knows exactly what is expected.

- A **measurable** goal is something that will either happen or not. If your goal is to earn $5 and you earn $4, you did not meet your goal.

- An **attainable** goal is realistic. Avoid goals that are highly unlikely. There is little value in expecting 1 million percent growth by next week.

- A **relevant** goal is one that will make a substantive difference to the team based on the team's ambitions. If your goal is to increase revenue by 25 percent year over year, you probably won't get there with a goal of making sure everyone has taken an equal share in cleaning the office coffee pot.

- A **timely** goal is tied to a schedule or has a deadline. Avoid creating goals that continue indefinitely into the future. After all, if you never say when you will accomplish the goal, don't you technically have the right to say you're "still working on it"?

- A **SMART** goal will ensure that your team knows exactly what they're working on, how they will measure their success, and when they should complete it, all while knowing the goal itself is both within reach and worth the time to pursue.

Set BIG goals

In addition to setting SMART goals, you should also seek to stretch the attainability of the goal as far out as you can. I'm referring to "the promised land," to Camelot, the triumph... not the weekly checklist. Jim Collins coined a term to describe what I'm talking about: Big Hairy Audacious Goal (BHAG). It's such a catchy phrase that I'm sure I'll never forget it, and I hope you don't, either. Everything should begin with that big and inspirational vision of where the team is ultimately going.

No one lauds the participation trophy, and there are no ticker-tape parades for teams that go 8-8 and then narrowly miss the playoffs. With few exceptions, no one is inspired by doing just okay.

Imagine standing up in front of your team and saying, "Team, this year we're going to do okay. We're going to make about as much money as last year. With any luck, the competition won't put us out of business." How inspired do you think they'd be? Talk about the impossible, or at a minimum, the unlikely. Set unreasonable (but still attainable) goals and convince your team that whether or not they're just within their reach, they're still worthy of pursuit. An essential part of being a leader is that you are worth following, and that means taking your team someplace interesting and invigorating along the way.

To accomplish big goals, set higher aspirations

Great leaders see the potential in everyone. They see a remarkable accomplishment waiting on the other side of commitment and hard work. They see the highest potential for individuals, often beyond what those people see for themselves. In this way, leadership is a gift you can give to others—the gift of seeing something in them that they could not see in themselves.

The first two questions I'll ask a team member in an early one-on-one meeting are:

1   What sort of work do you love doing; and
2   What sort of work do you hate doing?

I explain that knowing this information does not guarantee that I can give them dream assignments while removing everything they don't want to do. But it does allow me to shape how I work with each person to try and play to their strengths. I've also found that knowing what people love to do opens up your ability to see what's possible for them.

The world's greatest leaders aspire to see excellence in all things. They request that what was previously thought impossible be accomplished. They believe in your ability to do things that you don't think you can. Great leaders know that progress has never been the product of average aspirations. They know that a grand vision of the future will require more than satisfactory effort. They know that people are often their own biggest roadblocks to achieving their potential. Great leaders have fire and passion and expect their teams to rise up to the challenges and exceed their own perceived limitations in the pursuit of extraordinary accomplishments.

Hold your people accountable and do not let them quit. Provide the training and guidance to grow them into the people who can accomplish an audacious goal. View it as your personal responsibility to ensure your people become the best and most capable versions of themselves.

Set clear expectations

Gregg Popovich, the winningest coach in NBA history (regular season *and* playoffs) is well known for his leadership skills. Throughout his career, which spanned more than twenty years in San Antonio, Popovich's Spurs became famous for their precision and discipline, resulting in fewer mistakes than their opponents and a winning record to show for it. His players highlight his clarity of expectations as a hallmark trait. "When you step out on the court, not only you but every other player on the floor knows what he is asking of you," says Hall of Famer David Robinson, who retired in 2003.

Everyone, from coaches to CEOs to classroom teachers, relies on effective communication when leading a group. In any scenario where two or more people are working on the same goal, it's paramount that they each understand the other's plans. As a leader, you must ensure that the expectations for projects are clear and that the link between the expectations and how they relate to the bigger strategy and goals is clearly understood.

This requires a full-circle acceptance of the terms. Ask that the teammates articulate their understanding of the expectations, and then assert their commitment to and ownership of the assignment. But remember to sit on the same side of the table: expectations should be set in the context of a conversation, not a directive. For this circle to function properly, you must create the conditions for trust so that your team members have the freedom to be vulnerable and acknowledge when they do not understand.

I work hard with every team I'm a part of to establish relationships in which people can and feel comfortable enough to speak their minds. This creates the conditions for honest responses to questions like:

- Does that all make sense to everyone?

- Does everyone understand their roles and responsibilities? Now is the time to ask if you don't. This is important.

- Before we go any further, I need to make sure that everyone is on the same page. Does anyone have any concerns or confusion about the direction we're going?

Until you ask these questions and they are acknowledged, assume that the expectations are unclear and the prospect of success is in jeopardy. But know that if you clarify your expectations, you will be well on your way to success.

LOVABLE LEADER'S CHEAT SHEET

To lead with purpose, I will:

- Remember that purpose is not the same thing as "the reason."

- Lead the team to connect with a deeper purpose.

- Create a tangible destination by using SMART goals.

- Set big goals.

- Hold high aspirations and set clear expectations for my team.

THE MAP

Having identified your destination, you now need to figure out the route to get you there—and you're not going to rely on your GPS here. Strategy traces the route from your destination back to your starting point, creating a map from where you are to where you want to be.

Start at the End, Work Backward

Here's how I see building a strategy: Start with the goal. Then, analyze all the conditions that exist between your present state and that goal. This includes any of your challenges, the audiences and stakeholders you need to consider, the amount of time you have, and the resources you have at your disposal. Only when you've considered your goals and all the factors involved can you craft a good strategy.

We can look to the first *Iron Man* movie for a lesson in strategy. (This is my last superhero example, I promise.)

Tony Stark is captured and held hostage by a terrorist organization. They demand that he make them a weapon within a given time or meet his untimely end. He has to employ some crafty strategy to get out of there safely.

Let's start with his goal: Tony wants to escape his imprisonment before the deadline. He analyzes all the conditions of his present situation: he is unarmed, given sufficient raw materials to fulfill his captors' demands to their timeline, surrounded by hostile forces, and faced with an armory of weapons he himself had previously designed. However, what he does have is his extraordinary intellect and a kind ally in his fellow prisoner, Ho Yinsen, who could assist him in building the weapon his captors demand.

So, Tony begins to craft a plan: to use his design, engineering, and building talents not to build a weapon for his captors but instead to build a robotic suit made of metal, equipped with various weapons that allow him to dispense with his imprisoners and escape safely.

He designs the entire suit and then, piece by piece, builds the various components. When the suit is complete, he powers it up and executes his escape plan with only a few minor complications.

As with Tony Stark's suit, every good strategy should start with defining the goal, then analyzing the conditions, and finally designing a plan. You should follow this process for two reasons.

First, starting with the end is practical and makes planning a whole lot easier. Looking at the day-to-day steps and determining what that series of actions will add up to is a lot trickier than identifying where you are going and working backward at the step that directly precedes the end, followed by the step that precedes that one, and so on...

Second, considering the destination builds trust and clarity with your team. Choosing the right destination in the first place can help your teammates see your vision. When it aligns with theirs, you create the conditions for collaboration.

If your team can't get on board with the end goal, they may lose confidence in you. They may not believe in the way you're proposing to get there. The goal seems too unattainable. This is not a call to choose goals by consensus or to choose more reasonable goals. Quite the opposite. This is a call to create a vision for a big goal in the future—for example, to cut homelessness rates in half within three years, or win the championship this year and the next two years after that, or triple revenues over the next two years and launch a nonprofit.

Paint it as vividly as you can until all members of the team can see it clearly. This is also why you need to deeply understand your team, empathize with them, and relate to them on a personal level.

Knowing your team is also important when strategizing about roles and responsibilities. They are stakeholders and resources that will help you all reach the goal. If you deeply understand where each person excels and what they love to do, your strategy will be better thought out, your resources more carefully factored in, and, consequently, your chance of success exponentially increased.

Plans and Processes

Do you remember the first section header in chapter 3? No? Well, since it's been documented, you could always go back and check.

And that's the point.

Documentation is a fail-safe for your memory. It is a living artifact that contains the words to which you align your actions. With documentation, you are a team with a common playbook. Without it, you are aimless individuals, each operating from your unique recollections and spotty memories.

You need a clear strategy document that shows your goals, strategies, tactics, roles, and responsibilities. In order to ensure that your strategy is clear, make sure you ask for feedback, so you don't get stuck thinking you are clear when you're not.

Strategy documentation should be a collaborative process. Once you've created a plan, review it. Use the communications we discussed in chapter 5 to ensure your team understands and is aligned with the strategy. Bring everyone together for a strategy review so that everyone benefits from one another's involvement. This is a chance for people to raise issues, ask questions, or offer improvements. The goal is to leave the review with everyone feeling they are crystal-clear on the goals, the strategy, and their roles.

In addition to the plan, you also need a living handbook for your team. This should include all of your systems and processes, to be used by everyone on the team as a reference.

Many people think that process documentation ruins creativity by prescribing exact actions. But I have found that the more regimented and habitual processes become, the more freedom they allow. In his book *Good to Great*, Jim Collins said: "Disciplined people who engage in disciplined thought and who take disciplined action—operating with freedom within a framework of responsibilities—this is the cornerstone of a culture that creates greatness."

Process is discipline. Systems operate in the background, keeping things on track.

When you find a way to do something, document the steps. Be as granular as possible. This gets everyone moving in the same direction, using the same techniques. It encourages collaborative process improvement, with everyone working from the same toolkit. Goals are essential, and a great leader must also focus on the marginal process improvements that add up.

Tip: Manage your priorities. Your team, like all teams, will at some point have too many things to do. As a leader, you need to define the priorities, keeping your goals and strategies in mind, so that when your team is overwhelmed, you know how to best organize tasks to align with them.

If you can't figure out where to start, write down a list of everything that needs to be done, then prioritize it in numerical order. This is no time for indecision. Whatever is on that list gets done in that order.

Always Lock It In

The final step for plans, processes, and priorities is to make sure that you complete the process by getting buy-in. Do this for two reasons:

1 because commitments drive action; and
2 because genuine buy-in allows for genuine account-ability.

If you've involved your team in the planning process, then getting enthusiastic consent should not be too difficult. If someone gives you their honest word as a commitment to do something and they do not come through, hold them accountable. If they give their authentic commitment, then you know you have something to work with if they don't achieve their results. At least they are willing to try to improve.

There are a few ways I've found to confirm buy-in. You can ask:

- "Does that sound reasonable?"

- "Can we agree to this?"

- "How do you feel about these goals? Because if you think you can do it, this is what I'm going to hold you accountable to."

- "What do you need from me to ensure this gets done?"

Close the loop by ensuring that your team members agree to their part in the plan.

LOVABLE LEADER'S CHEAT SHEET

To develop excellent strategies, I will:

- Remember that the best-executed strategies begin with aligned goals.

- Start with the end and work backward.

- Involve my team in the creation of strategies to deepen their ownership.

- Document our plans to provide clarity to the team and increase accountability.

- Help the team understand and manage priorities.

- Increase accountability across the entire team by locking in commitments, because commitments drive action, and genuine buy-in allows for genuine accountability.

THE JOURNEY

Once you have determined where you're going
(your destination) and how you're getting
there (your strategy), you embark upon the journey.
This is where ideas and words manifest in action.
This is the daily practice of leadership.

NOW THAT your plans are in place, it's time to buckle up for the journey ahead. If you've followed all of the steps in this book so far, you should be feeling good at this point:

- You have built trust with each team member, and they've built trust with one another.

- You have defined the team and set expectations with the eight commitments.

- You have defined your purpose and engaged your team to align with common values.

- You have set your destination/goals with specific time-lines and measurements.

- You have created and documented the plans to accomplish your goals.

Now it's time to walk the walk. On the road ahead, you'll want to be mindful of four practices:

1 Maintaining strong team bonds;
2 Managing for motivation;
3 Practicing balanced oversight; and
4 Staying flexible to navigate change.

Here's how to manage the journey.

Maintain Strong Team Bonds

No matter how well you define your team at the outset or how specific your defined commitments are, you will still need to nurture and maintain your team bonds. Even the strongest bonds weaken under enough stress or pressure. How teams navigate tumultuous times is a better indicator of their potential than how they manage success.

In order to maintain strong team bonds, you must reinforce the commitments of your team by setting a good example and living those commitments, but also by holding others on the team accountable. It's also important to remember that while you cannot force anyone to grow, you can foster an environment and support the kind of culture that creates ideal conditions where growth is a natural consequence.

Love and care for your people, as shown through encouragement and protection, is the most direct route for creating powerful relationships, strong team bonds, and resilience.

Imagine if at the end of a diversity, equity, and inclusion workshop, instead of wrapping up and getting back to the workday, the leader of the company stood up and said:

> I want everyone on this team to know this: you matter, and this organization will stand behind you 100 percent of the time. Harm will not be tolerated. If anyone in this organization experiences anything that makes them feel unsafe, threatened, or discriminated against by anyone—whether they are in this room or they are clients—it will be dealt with, and we will defend you above all else. There is no client, team member, or revenue goal more important than your safety, well-being, and belonging in this organization. You can expect this from us, and we in turn expect this from all of you. We stand with each other.

Adopt this posture and galvanize your team to do the same. This way of operating must become the default; then, team members will be more likely to step in and help each other, stand up to protect one another, and move in unison toward that common goal.

When you think about building your team, you're not simply growing better teammates. You're growing a new crop of leaders. One of the more important intuitions you can develop is the ability to recognize people's strengths and weaknesses, and to understand their motivations. Not everyone wants to be in the spotlight; not everyone will desire to be an outspoken leader; and some people may take longer to learn things. Being able to recognize people's natural abilities, accepting everyone for who they are, and having the patience to accept the different speeds at which people make an impact are all invaluable skills in building strong team bonds based on trust.

Tip: Always judge based on strengths. An old, wise proverb states, "Everybody is a genius. But if you judge a fish by its ability to climb a tree, it will live its whole life believing that it is stupid." This quote is typically attributed to Albert Einstein, though that has been disputed. Whoever came up with it was on to something. Too often, people mistake something *they* can do easily as something *everyone* can do without effort. As a leader, you must understand that everyone has their strengths and weaknesses. It is not your job to change those so much as it is to accentuate the strengths and minimize the weaknesses. In some cases, your job will be to work with your teammate to improve upon their weaknesses. However, you must be careful to judge your teammates on their strengths rather than their weaknesses.

Manage for Motivation

Great leaders are driven by purpose, and they excite and motivate their teams with their passion. They always plan to succeed but accept that sometimes they won't. Following in the footsteps of the greatest leaders, strive to possess unyielding belief and "broad shoulders" to motivate your team.

As a leader, your energy should be contagious. If you believe you can do it, you are far more likely to accomplish your goal. Great leaders understand the importance of seeing something bigger and rally their teams with belief that it is possible. You may still have doubts and bad days, and you may yet question your ability from time to time. Of course. All great leaders do. Despite that, you must find a way to manufacture belief for yourself and your team. You must summon the will to get back up after being knocked down.

When Kevin Love joined Gary Vaynerchuk on his podcast, *The GaryVee Audio Experience*, he recounted a story about how LeBron James inspired the 3–1 NBA Finals comeback. Love told Vaynerchuk that before the turnaround game, "Bron said, he looked around and said, 'You know what guys? It's written. We're going to win tomorrow night. We're going to have a huge game. It's going to be tough. It's going to come down to the last few minutes. We're not losing at home. Game 7, anything can happen.' That's how it played out. It still gives me chills thinking about it."

If you're a sports fan, you probably have a list of favorite performances whereby a player "gets in the zone" and scores enough points to carry the team to victory, seemingly by themselves. You've probably also seen the losing coach stand up at the press conference and assume 100 percent of the blame for the loss. In both winning and losing situations, true leaders step up and demand of themselves that, no matter what happens, the results rest squarely on their shoulders. Is this logically true? No! In any team situation, the responsibility is shared. However, as you know, leaders carry the burden of responsibility.

Tip: Understand intrinsic and extrinsic motivation. We touched on these types of motivation earlier. As a refresher, we fundamentally have two different states of motivation: intrinsic and extrinsic. Extrinsic motivators come from the outside. They could be money, attention, awards, and much more. Intrinsic motivators are internal. They could be pride, shame, lust, excitement, ambition, and other emotions. Harnessing the power of extrinsic motivators is useful, but the results tend to be short-lived, easily replaceable, and vulnerable to competitive forces. If you can tap into intrinsic motivators, you will channel long-lasting and deeply meaningful engagement for your team. Both are valuable, and both have their place.

To extrinsically motivate people, think in terms of tangible "rewards." Talk to your people about their growth and their goals. Be careful, however. Once you fall into the pattern of offering extrinsic rewards, you may get locked into a situation where people become less motivated in the absence of reward. While extrinsic rewards have their place, intrinsic rewards may be more effective and less costly. To intrinsically motivate people, focus on feedback and genuine praise.

Practice Balanced Oversight

Although you must get your hands dirty from time to time, your primary role as a leader is to support the action of those under your care and guidance. This requires your attention, patience, and occasional check-in.

Many leaders go astray by micromanaging. Micromanagement is a product of a desire for meticulous control, sometimes because of overzealous ownership of a project, sometimes because of concern that the project won't be done properly or on time. In any case, micromanagement clearly signals that you lack trust in your team. Trust is the seed of ownership. If you do not trust your people, they cannot take ownership.

While it may be faster for you to write the strategy or step in to save the sales call or show the project manager how the software works, all that does is create more work. For the team member who needs to grow, you've robbed them of the opportunity to fail and learn. For the team member who is ready to take on the work, you've shown them that you lack confidence in them. Stop saving the day—start giving your team a chance to be the heroes.

Create the right environment to ensure that everyone on your team feels ownership. Train your people to think like an owner, and be a leader rather than stepping in and doing the job for them or hovering over their shoulders. Don't lead by training people what to do. Lead by training people how to see things.

Stay Flexible to Navigate Change

No matter how solid your plans or how capable your team, things will come up that will rattle the ground beneath your feet. Clients may leave, opponents and competitors may ambush you, or the market conditions could shift in a flash. You must expect such changes. This way, they are less likely to take you by surprise. Expect them and, whenever possible, plan for them—and prepare your team to manage unforeseeable change, too. Role-playing and involving them in real situations of change can help with this.

Role-playing is creating no-stakes situations for your team members to practice how they might handle unforeseen changes as they arise. It provides a safe environment in which to develop problem-solving skills. It also gives your team members practice making important decisions in the moment. Ideally, the first time someone has the freedom to decide would not be in the middle of a crisis. Each team member needs to feel confident that they have the trust of their leadership team to adapt to changes.

What does role-play look like?

- A package manufacturing firm role-plays supply chain bottlenecks or sudden requests to speed up so the project manager has a chance to move things around quickly to make the timeline work for the client.

- A PR firm picks a random day and team member each week and introduces a functional crisis scenario with a real client. See how well the team member builds or executes a crisis management plan.

- A financial services firm runs the scenario of a market crash, and has associates call one another to practice having a conversation with the client.

Go through the motions and develop some familiarity and comfort with the process. When a real change does come up, make sure to engage your team members in the solution so that they continually build the mental and emotional muscles to navigate change in the future. Don't just leave them on the sidelines watching you work. This is part of building your muscle for leadership. Even if things are tense, asking a team member what they would do gives them the opportunity to showcase what they've learned and to grow in their own leadership.

People typically find the emotional side of navigating change more difficult than tactical planning around it. Unfortunately, the emotional distress of change can sometimes impede people's ability to think clearly and strategize new solutions. But, there is one invaluable tool for dealing with the emotional side of navigating change.

Negative thinking

A popular practice among the great Stoic philosophers was known as negative thinking. When you encounter a situation that arouses anxiety, going deeply into that rabbit hole of concern can be helpful. Think through how bad things could get. Imagine the client leaving, them suing you, losing your home. Go all the way to the bottom. What you'll typically realize is this: most of that is highly unlikely, and most of those fears are unjustified.

When I started my agency in 2010, I was routinely terrified of becoming homeless. Despite having clients and growing the business every year, I had a recurring fear that all of my clients would leave, I'd never get work again, I'd look for a job too late, and I'd wind up evicted and sleeping on the streets with my dog. I'm not being hyperbolic here. This was a real fear, and it was one I had almost every week without any good reason.

One morning in 2014, my friend Naomi came over for coffee before work. We got to chatting, and I casually mentioned this recurring fear of mine and how it drove me to work hard every day. She looked at me and seemed genuinely confused and maybe even a little disappointed. After what felt like an entire minute went by, I asked, "What?" Her answer became the punchline of the power of negative thinking in my life. "Jeff, if all of that happened, you could just come and sleep on our couch until you get back on your feet."

And that was when I began to realize that the fears that we make up in our head are not the truth. They are anxiety-induced fantasies where everything that could go wrong does go wrong, and we are all alone... but we're not.

You can use this knowledge with your team in two important ways. First, when something comes up—let's say a major event that immediately, drastically cuts an organization's income—discussing it openly, including an exploration of the absolute worst-case scenario, prepares everyone for it and for what they can do to make sure that the darkest possibilities never happen. It also gives everyone the opportunity to create a strategy for navigating the worst-case scenario together. Maybe everyone agrees to take a pay cut so that no one is laid off. Maybe everyone agrees to put more hours in at the office, make more sales calls, or work a few more hours. Discussing the worst-case scenario gives everyone a chance to confront it and work through their emotional response to it with the support of the group. This sort of transparency also builds trust.

Negative thinking can also be useful for proactively coming up with positive solutions. Because humans tend toward a strong negative bias, it's often easier to think about everything that could go wrong before painting a picture of everything going right.

Let's say you needed to figure out the best way to generate more revenue from existing clients. Reframe the objective in the negative, asking, "What is the best way to lose revenue from existing clients?" or "What is the worst way to generate more revenue from existing clients?" The answers to that question might be things like:

- Be unresponsive to their calls and emails.

- Neglect to ask them about additional work.

- Be impatient with them.

- Miss deadlines.

To get to a solution that would increase the likelihood of generating more revenue from existing clients, you invert the negative responses. New strategies might include:

- Be ultra-responsive to their calls and emails.

- Regularly ask them about additional work.

- Be patient with them and provide extra documentation.

- Hit all deadlines and build a dashboard so that the client can see the output of deliverables by due date.

Negative thinking is a tool that can be remarkably helpful for building a creative and resilient team in the face of inevitable changes.

LOVABLE LEADER'S CHEAT SHEET

To excel at the daily practice of leadership, I will:

- Maintain strong team bonds by reinforcing the commitments of the team.

- Appreciate each individual by judging them on their strengths, not their weaknesses.

- Manage with the intent to motivate.

- Maintain an unwavering belief in my team.

- Step up and carry the additional weight whenever I'm needed.

- Practice balanced oversight.

- Stay flexible to navigate change.

- Embrace the power of negative thinking to stay grounded.

9

THE DETOURS

Leadership will not always go according to plan. You will make mistakes. Your patience and resilience will be tested. You will want to ignore the problems or avoid them but you already know that won't help. So, you've got to plan for detours.

LET'S SAY that you follow this entire playbook. As a leader, you do everything in your power to create a culture of trust. You take the time to paint your team a marvelous and vivid portrait for the inspiring future. On your journey toward that future, you ensure safe travels. Throughout all of this, your care for the team is self-evident.

You will still encounter problems. You will have team members who do not like you, do not respect you, do not buy into the vision. You will have team members who do not like one another.

Be well prepared for the uncomfortable conversations that lie ahead, regardless of how the problems present. Conflict in life is inevitable. Most of us don't seek it out or find it comfortable. But it's important to recognize that conflict represents an important moment in any relationship, and how we handle it can define the entire future of that relationship. Therefore, we should not avoid conflict. Instead, as I mentioned in chapter 4, we should embrace conflict to ensure that it is productive.

In this chapter, I'm going to arm you with a variety of different frameworks to deal with challenges that arise on your team. And we'll look at the realistic, albeit hypothetical, example of Jeremy, who presents a classic challenge.

Jeremy is a nice guy, but he's moody. He tends to be pessimistic and unnecessarily play devil's advocate. Far too often, he finds himself overwhelmed and stressed out when his workload increases. He's extremely talented but, lately, he just seems like he's given up. He's been missing assignment due dates, and the quality of his work seems like he's just phoning it in.

Recently, several team members have privately approached his lovable leader about Jeremy's behavior. He's been passive-aggressive with several people. On top of that, they say he's been bad-mouthing the leader, specifically to some of the newer employees and interns. He's older than the lovable leader and he has had a bit of a condescending attitude about having to report to them. It's clear that he thought the promotion to leader would be his.

Deal with Problems

Unfortunately, instead of dealing with problems on the team, too many leaders just let people go and start over. In theory, it *is* easier to just get rid of someone who isn't pulling their weight or who is dragging down the rest of the team. In reality, though, it can be costly.

In business, every team member who is let go and replaced is a substantial expense. Aside from the loss of knowledge, finding talent can be costly not just because of the money but also because of the time and cultural implications:

- Being down a team member puts additional stress on others to pick up the slack. This can result in missed opportunities because of insufficient resources.

- The dollar costs of recruitment and promotion of job placements can add up quickly.

- The time spent interviewing candidates, making offers, and onboarding new team members could be spent elsewhere.

Though I am pointing out the potential cost of letting someone go, I'm not suggesting you *must* keep every employee, of course. Sometimes the cost of keeping someone vastly exceeds the cost of replacing them. There are definitely instances when the wrong team member is brought on and they are a bad fit for the culture. There are instances of people, in their current situation, being "uncoachable" and unwilling to change. There are even, inexplicably, those metaphorical arsonists who deliberately set fires to their team with little remorse because they enjoy the chaos. It should be obvious that tolerating someone like this is unacceptable.

All of this is to illustrate that there are a lot of factors, and it's complicated. The most important thing is to develop your ability to see things clearly. To do this, you must cultivate the emotional intelligence and patience to start by asking yourself these questions: Can this problem be resolved? Can this "liability" be turned into an "asset"?

This is vital because how you handle problems sends a signal to every person on your team. If you rush to fire someone, or avoid doing the work to adequately understand the issues and resolve problems, then the rest of the team may worry about their role and feel unsafe. People cannot work at their best when they fear for their job.

Unfortunately, this is the part of the book where we have to acknowledge that try as you might, your team will encounter problems, and you will need to deal with it. Try as you might to sit on the same side of the table, you will only be able to help those who are willing to work with you. At the end of this chapter, we'll talk more about when to fire someone and the steps to take when doing so.

While sitting on the same side of the table is always the best place to start, sometimes you'll need to take the opposite approach: sitting across the table.

Tip: Avoid manipulation. The section you are about to read is filled with tactics for productive conflict resolution. Sometimes these sound a lot like manipulation, but as you will likely guess, that's not what I'm advocating for. The intention of these techniques is to build stronger relationships, reach productive outcomes, and reduce harm. *Never* lie, coerce, intimidate, or otherwise use the skills you've acquired to make anyone feel unsafe, threatened, or limit their agency to make choices. Interactions may get uncomfortable at times, and in some cases, you should acknowledge that, understand it, and seek to use that tension to create positive outcomes.

Intensity Over Anger

In most cases, you should seek to avoid escalating a situation. However, sometimes it is necessary. When you must escalate, avoid giving in to the instinct to raise your voice, and instead increase your intensity.

Many people signal their frustration by showcasing the full range of their emotions. This can take the form of yelling, screaming, and even acts of physicality, such as tossing papers or slamming hands on a table. Raising your voice is a sign that you have lost control, that you have given in and cannot handle the situation calmly and professionally.

A lovable leader never needs to raise their voice; there are other ways to make an emotional impact on someone. Intensity can be communicated through words, tone, use of silence, facial expressions, and body language. Most importantly, though, you must be steady in your emotions. Sometimes looking intently at someone and asking a single-pointed question can land with substantially more weight than raising your voice ever could.

Remember Jeremy, our pessimistic devil's advocate? More than a handful of leaders would confront him and express their anger with his behavior, perhaps in a private meeting or even in front of other team members.

A lovable leader might approach the situation differently. A lovable leader is aware of when their ego is hurt. Instead of reacting, they plan conversations that will be intense and effective. A lovable leader might plan a private, in-person meeting with Jeremy. In this meeting, the lovable leader would make Jeremy comfortable and then use a direct, confronting question to throw him off balance and build tension in the room.

A lovable leader must stand firm

Many will read the title of this book and assume that lovable leadership is all about rainbows, stickers, and soft-serve ice cream with sprinkles. Lovable leadership is built atop positive experiences, compassion, empathy, and kindness, but we are not operating in a vacuum here. You will not always be able to "hug it out." So while you must remain compassionate, empathetic, and kind, you also must have the requisite skills to effectively stand your ground, defend your positions, and deal with disrespect. If you find that you are being disrespected, you have not yet attained your goal.

Respect is a subjective experience, so we should outline what it means to be disrespected and differentiate that from unacceptable levels of performance. For instance:

- Questioning your directions does not imply disrespect, but questioning your integrity does.

- Not following an instruction or neglecting to complete a task is not necessarily disrespectful. Actively coordinating your team against you behind your back is.

- Mistakes are not inherently disrespectful. People are human beings, and mistakes will be made. Even a recurring error is not a sign of disrespect. However, mistakes that result from a dismissive attitude and approach toward your guidance and leadership are disrespectful.

In the context of these lessons, disrespect has more to do with how one approaches the relationship and the work than it does with the output or deliverables of the work.

Use Deafening Silence

One of the most powerful techniques you can learn is mastering the art of silence. Silence can be awkward. It can be stressful. It can be anxiety-inducing. People run from silence. They talk to fill the space. They shift uncomfortably in their seat as silence lingers in the air.

Good!

When you control the silence, you control the conversation. This can give you immense power in a conversation, especially one where you need to gain leverage.

For example:

- When you ask a question and then sit comfortably in the silence, it puts you squarely in control of the flow of conversation. It also creates tension. You basically force the other person to eventually answer.

- Sitting in silence after someone speaks can be very disruptive to them. We are used to reasonably quick responses. The silence may give the impression that you are offended, upset, or didn't understand. They will often scramble to fill the silence.

- When people feel uncomfortable in silence, they often begin blabbing just to avoid the discomfort. You may learn valuable information this way.

- Silence heightens attention. When you punctuate your sentences with silence, it draws the other party in.

- You can also use silence when giving instructions. Insert a pause before making a substantive point, to draw them in. During the silence, look them in the eyes.

Ask Questions

What happens when you ask a question?

Did you notice how you instinctively began thinking about the answer? Did you want to know the answer before I said it? Be honest, did you think about the answer?

Yes or no, you're only further proving the point. When our brains hear a question, they automatically kick into gear trying to answer it. This is amazingly powerful. As I said earlier, when you ask the questions, you dictate the flow of the conversation. You can control the tone, pace, and direction of any conversation simply through the use of carefully posed questions.

If you are dealing with a conflict, do not underestimate the power of questions. Here are a handful you can use to gather more information:

- Why?
- What makes you say that?
- What else can you say about that?
- What would you do if you were in my position?
- How do you think that might make your teammate feel?
- What are your next steps?

These are just a few, but the goal is to put the conversation back in their hands, and keep them talking. In each of these situations, you are getting the other party to help solve the problem or talk their way into identifying other problems.

Now, without looking ahead, what do you think the third method of intensity is?

Did I get you thinking about the answer again?

Be Clear and Reasonable

In the desire to raise your intensity, you may feel the need to increase the gravity of the consequences or reinforce your title to give you more leverage.

That is a mistake.

Never make idle threats or appeal to your perceived authority to move a conversation toward a resolution. Instead, double down on the commitments of a lovable team—most notably, the commitments to

- thoughtful, kind communication
- alignment
- ownership

You are not engaged in a contest of will. You are not trying to win a fight. You did not sit down for this uncomfortable conversation to assert your org-chart dominance. You did it to resolve an issue. So, you need to return to your commitments and set an example. You are trying to get back into alignment. Be clear about your goals and why you're there. Listen to the other person's side of the story and ensure that what you're asking for is clear and reasonable in the context of their experience.

Own the Moral High Ground

Owning the moral high ground is an attempt to remove any possible justification for a teammate's response when pressed about a lack of activity or results.

To illustrate how this works, let's use the example of taking out the trash that we talked about earlier. Let's assume that taking out the trash is a shared responsibility among the team. If over the course of a twenty-day work month, five team members ideally take out the trash four days and you took out the trash eleven days, you would be in a reasonable position, above reproach. If, on top of that, you brought in 75 percent of the company's revenue, stepped in to help all four of your team members with their work, and bought lunch for the entire office, you are further insulated from criticism.

When you find yourself in the middle of an uncomfortable, difficult conversation, you have an advantage of being armed with the knowledge that you have done the very same work you were asking your teammate to do, taken the ownership you encourage them to take, and spoken with the thoughtfulness, kindness, and respect that you expect. This is further magnified by the reality that you likely have more responsibilities to attend to than the people who report to you.

If you can be a brilliant example, you will be afforded new opportunities to subtly shine a spotlight on the disparity between what was agreed to and what happened.

Forced Empathy

Assuming that you're practicing the other steps in this book, you already actively listen and empathize. You should have a good idea of the other person's story before you sit down to talk. If you sense that they are having trouble grasping the reason for a conversation about course correction, the best thing to do is to switch places, metaphorically: "What would you do if you were me right now? How would you handle the situation?"

That's the most basic way of doing it. Even more impactful is to thoroughly describe the problem that spurred this discussion, explain what your goals are, and then ask them to resolve it. Back to Jeremy, here's what his lovable leader might say:

> Jeremy, you know how important it is for us to operate as a team. I've seen a few instances when you've given your teammates passive-aggressive and sarcastic feedback, which some people could read as condescending. At the same time, according to our company dashboard, I also see that your production is the lowest it has ever been. I love having you on the team, and I can see that something has been bothering you, yet I can't seem to get out of you what's wrong. Put yourself in my shoes. You've got a team member that you really care about, that you know is a star performer who is underperforming, and you see that their behavior is starting to impact the mood of our team. What would you do in my position to get everything back on track?

Forced empathy only works if you own some portion of the moral high ground. For example, Jeremy could respond to his leader with: "Well, if we're talking about people who are impatient and sarcastic, why aren't we talking about you? And while we're on the subject, it must be nice to sit on the sidelines and judge my production when every time I ask you for help, you're either too busy or just flat out talk down to me."

If you want to be able to use the forced empathy technique, then when the other person puts themselves in your shoes, they need to see themselves as someone whom they aspire to be like, or, at least, who is reasonable and hardworking.

The disappointment of a one-way street

I don't remember how old I was, but I had lied to my father about something. When he found out, he told me that he was disappointed and that I would need to earn back his trust. That is the last time I can recall lying. That "d-word" is weighted like an anvil. In general, we all want to be the best versions of ourselves. We want to impress those around us. We want to be important. We are also most reluctant to screw over the people who are on our side.

In the same way that disappointing my father led me to a life of honesty, leaders can change bad behavior by turning on the street lights to illuminate a one-way street.

Imagine a continuation of the conversation with Jeremy, when he accuses his leader of all manner of sarcasm, judgment, and the like. Now let's rest assured that all of those accusations are patently false. The lovable leader, by all other accounts, is kind and patient. Here's how the one-way street might play out after that:

> I hear what you're saying, and I apologize that you've felt I wasn't there to support you. My calendar is available to the entire team, and it sounds like I didn't do enough to communicate that to you. For that, I'm sorry. That said, I'm a little disappointed that the conversation has gone in this direction. My intention in sitting down with you was to get us realigned. I'm committed to your growth in this organization, and I have no desire to argue with you. I'm trying to be on the same team here, and right now, I don't get the feeling that you share that commitment. If you give me the benefit

of the doubt in the same way that I'm trying to give
you the benefit of the doubt, can you understand how
I might see things that way?

The subtext of this is: "I'm on your side. It's a shame that
you're not on mine." It implies that they could resolve the
issue if only Jeremy would come to the negotiating table.

Again, this only works if you own the moral high
ground. Tyrannical bosses have no leverage other than
organizational and hierarchical threats. Real power happens when people willingly line up to support your vision,
not when they're operating under coercion.

Play the Same Game

A challenge you're likely to experience in conflict-resolution conversations is that they go off on tangents,
often unintentionally. Staying on message is important.
In media training, people are typically instructed to stay
on topic, to be prepared and keep their cool, no matter
what type of question an interviewer throws their way.
The same is true for a conflict-resolution discussion. You
must stay on topic, focus on your objective, and stick to
it, to see it through to the resolution.

Like most conversations, the tough ones will have a
beginning, middle, and end. These are the three places
to ensure that both parties are on the same page about
the purpose of the conversation and any other criteria to
make sure no one is talking past one another.

To start, you might ask for consent to have the conversation: "I'd like to talk about your performance. I've noticed some issues, and I'd like for us to use this time to speak productively about how we can solve them. Does that sound reasonable to you?"

In the middle, you might check in: "How are you feeling? Do you feel like we're on the right track?"

At the end, you'll want to close the loop: "Okay, so with everything that we've discussed, are you on board and aligned with the plan?"

Leverage Intermediaries

Sometimes you need a messenger who will talk to the person you're having a problem with, to be a voice of reason. Not everyone is going to like you. Not everyone is going to recognize your value, regardless of how much you do or how visible or invisible that work is.

As a leader, you will be met with resistance from time to time, no matter how lovable you are or what a great communicator you are. Because to be led by another often requires a willingness to sacrifice the ego. Not everyone takes this well. Perhaps you come in as an outsider. As an example, think of how children often relate to a new stepparent. Perhaps you'll be resisted. In some cases, your personality may not mesh with certain members of your team.

Do not take this personally and do not try and climb this mountain alone. Often, the most effective strategy when you encounter resistance is to make an ally who is trusted by the person resisting you.

In some cases, you will need a neutral or warm third party to help you progress. This can be true when dealing with your team members or clients. An endorsement from a third party can be a powerful thing—you're able to leverage the trust and social capital they've gained. This should be someone with whom the resistor already has social equity, whereas you may have none. If you have no trust in the bank from which to make a withdrawal, it is essential to leverage the social capital of others.

While HR is a third-party option, it's typically not a particularly good option. HR represents the interests of the company, not the employee. You're looking to leverage relationship equity. This means understanding the social circles that exist within an organization. Friendships are made at work, and alliances among colleagues will naturally form. This is where you want to go in search of an intermediary who can help. Involving HR can sometimes make things feel far more formal and consequential. If the ideal intermediary also happens to work in HR, you can still choose them, but again, what you're primarily looking for is someone with whom you have a relationship, and who also has a relationship with the person you need to deal with. You need someone who can lend you some of their social equity by vouching for you. Remember, you're not using this person, you're leveraging them for a positive outcome. Make sure that their participation leaves them better off in both relationships: the one with you and the one with the person you need to improve your relationship with.

Stacking Principles for Ultimate Leverage

Each of these principles I've described, when used discretely, will help correct a situation. Combining them can act as a force multiplier. In a conversation, the more leverage you need to get things back on track, the more of these principles and other strategies from this book you'll want to combine.

For instance, you could ask questions to control the flow of the conversation and use deafening silence while waiting for the answers. You could then follow it up with clear and reasonable requests, trying to lock it in with "Does this sound reasonable? Can we agree to this?" If they don't accept, try using forced empathy, asking, "What would you do if you were in my position?" If the conversation goes off track, make sure to keep bringing it back to your objective. If the struggles continue, lean on the moral high ground that you've built, and point out the one-way street saying something like, "I hope you can see how hard I'm trying to make this work. I really value having you on the team, and I'm honestly a little disappointed that I can't seem to figure out how to get you as invested in resolving the issue as I am."

If you've done the work from previous chapters, such as enrolling the team member in the commitments of the team, ensuring everyone understands productive conflict, and making expectations clear, you have a variety of different directions in which you can take the conversation to realign.

Time to Hit Eject

Every leader will inevitably have to go through it. At some point, you'll ask yourself, "Where is the line before you get rid of someone or give up on them?" I cannot definitively answer that for you because each scenario is different. Here are a few guidelines I adhere to. Remove someone from the team if they have:

- Given up and shown no interest in turning things around;

- Displayed constant hostility toward you or other team members;

- Poisoned the well by creating unmanageable friction on the team; or

- Taken deliberate actions to sabotage the team.

Before you act, make sure that you fully understand how things came to this.

Whenever you have to remove someone from the team, try to do so with as little harm to them as possible. This benefits you by showing the team you care even when things don't work out. It also allows you to potentially preserve a relationship that may not have worked out for reasons beyond either of your control. Sometimes, it's just a bad fit.

In a professional setting, you could write a LinkedIn recommendation, offer to do an interview coaching session, or introduce them to other companies that may have open positions. This is one more instance of coming back to kindness and respect.

Whatever you do, do it because extending your care to those who are leaving your team is almost as important as how you treat those who are currently on your team.

LOVABLE LEADER'S CHEAT SHEET

When things go wrong with my team, I will:

- Try to fix problems rather than get rid of them.

- Raise intensity instead of my voice by:
  - Using silence strategically.
  - Asking questions.
  - Being clear and reasonable.

- Be ready for a productive conversation built on the foundation of my moral high ground.

- Make sure to stay on topic so the issue can be resolved.

- Leverage intermediaries to open the door for a productive conversation.

- Care for people even when I have to remove them from my team.

THE BALANCE

Maintaining balance as you lead is critical. Avoid extremes on the journey—too controlling and you'll quash creativity and innovation, too lax and your team will feel directionless—but the moment you think you've got it figured out, you'll find an exception. Stay open, stay humble, experiment, and find what works for you.

IN THE phase of my career before I'd adopted a leadership mindset, and in roles that confer leadership responsibilities, I found that many of the managers I directly reported to tended to gravitate toward one extreme or another. In some cases, they were painfully authoritarian, and in other cases, I watched as people dismissed them as pushovers and walked all over them. I noticed how any time one of my managers opened his mouth, I could be reasonably sure that he was levying criticism. He was very different from the manager who never had a bad thing to say about anyone or anything, who was an unrelenting cheerleader even when what the team needed was course correction.

In my own leadership roles, I've often noticed how difficult it is to not "over-rotate" in a desire to avoid coming across a certain way. I went through a period when I was adamant about not being a dictator, so I made sure to always engage my team and ask for ideas. But I took it too far. We started missing deadlines, or going through easily avoidable mistakes because I refused to assert myself, even when it was the right move. I tend to be optimistic, but in my leadership roles, that has sometimes put me in a position where the team has been ill-prepared. I assumed everything would go according to plan and refused to acknowledge how much work really needed to be done. My optimistic posture made me naive.

Great leadership is always a balance that stops the inevitable slide into the extremes. In most cases, leaders will find themselves choosing between two options in an either/or framing. Commonly, you might ask whether you should be

- unilateral versus collaborative
- high control versus laissez-faire
- optimistic versus naive
- strict versus lenient
- praiseful versus critical

Rarely is a situation truly about either/or, but it is often about understanding the balance between two opposing ends of a spectrum, and the ideal mix in the middle. Let's explore balance each of these spectrums.

Unilateral versus Collaborative

Who makes the decisions? Should it be you, or should it be your team? This is not an either/or decision. In some circumstances, you should make the decision on your own, but you should *always* be mindful of how a decision impacts the team. For example, a client wants to move the deadline for a project up by one week. This is an important client, and their contract alone helps pay two people's salaries. So, what do you do? You are the leader. This is your privilege, burden, and responsibility. Think about the impact on your team, but also think about how this may affect the relationship with the client. This is a tough decision. Make the call.

Similarly, plenty of decisions absolutely should be made collectively. An aligned team is unlikely to make a decision the leader would not approve of. Let's imagine that you are looking to hire a new team member. You have a small, six-person team, and there are currently three strong applicants in their final round of interviews. When it comes to making the final decision, your team needs to be involved. They need to tell you why they like one candidate over another. They need to share what skills they think are most important. The culture of your team is critical for the performance and health of your team. Don't risk a gut decision without making sure that it isn't in conflict with how your team sees things.

Balance exists when, regardless of who makes the decision, it carefully considers what you, as the leader, would do, while also accounting for the impact on the rest of the team.

Your team is not going to like every decision you make, but if they understand how you make decisions and they trust you, knowing that you care about each of them, they will defer to your judgment. You're not going to like every collaborative decision, but if you trust that your team is aligned and that they respect your perspective, then you should defer to their judgment.

A strong team shares values and purpose, and therefore, whether you, someone else, or the team decides, everyone should be able to align with it.

High Control versus Laissez-Faire

There are three types of events in this world: events you can control, events you can influence, and events you can do nothing about but accept.

Don't confuse these or mistakenly believe that you can control much. It will only make you angry. Life has a funny way of shaking that belief to the ground. Likewise, don't fall victim to believing you have to accept much in this world. More often than not, you can stand up and influence an event. Improving your ability to distinguish between these types of events is important.

If a team member at work is constantly coming in late in the morning:

- **Control** could look like a verbal warning followed by formal disciplinary measures and possibly termination. It could also look like offering accountability calls, or giving this person a ride to work in the morning.

- **Influence** could look like finding common goals to align with and working together to address the underlying problem that being late may create for the team.

- **Acceptance** could be letting the team member continue to come in late and letting the team know why the exception is being made.

None of these approaches is inherently right or wrong. They are just different methods of dealing with a situation. However, when determining which is the right approach for a given situation consider this... You can only control situations in which there are no other significant competing forces—and these situations are few and far between. As a result, you can typically control situations only where your own behavior and actions are in question. Seek to control situations only where the stakes, stress, or complexity are high and where exerting yourself has a low risk of unintended consequences. For instance, your team may look to you to step up and take control when a decision needs to be made under a tight timeline. You may want to take over a sales meeting when it comes time to close. Control is, more often than not, an illusion, and your desire to attempt to control should be kept to a minimum.

Often, where control may be your first instinct, influence will be a much more appropriate response. Rather than trying to exert your authority to get someone to change their behavior, you will find much more success if you can influence them to change gradually. Influence is more appropriate in any situation where there are multiple competing forces or where being too heavy-handed can produce unintended consequences. If a situation looks hopeless, and you feel as though acceptance is your only option, ask yourself whether there is any chance for you to make an impact. If the answer is yes, then you should continue to try to influence the situation.

Acceptance should be reserved for those scenarios where even influence would be overstepping your boundaries, or where either control or influence would be futile. Too often leaders get drunk on authority and feel as though they need to have an opinion on everything in their field of vision.

While you will always have the options to control, influence, or accept, I recommend you lean toward influence. In general, the best long-term solution is to help your team members grow so that they are better able to help themselves in the future. Great leaders often look for an individual's natural ability and leverage those abilities to help them to grow as a leader on the team.

According to a study by the University of Birmingham's business school, a survey of 20,000 employees found that the primary factor in job satisfaction is autonomy. The more control exerted over an employee, the lower the job satisfaction. Despite this, leaders still choose to exert varying degrees of control over their team members because they believe it to be the most effective strategy.

Some leaders crave power and submission. They take a hands-on approach to ensure that their vision is being implemented according to plan. For these types of leaders, team members are cogs in a machine. They are utilitarian, often replaceable. The leader and their plan (and ego) are the real stars of the show. Avoid this approach.

At the other end, some leaders adopt a laissez-faire approach. They believe in letting people make mistakes so they can learn from them. Depending on the other aspects of the person's leadership, this can be very effective or fail miserably. It really falls on how well they support in the moments of failure and build a culture around learning.

Optimistic versus Naive

Believing in your people is a good thing, as is optimism about your team's chances of success. Being blind to reality is a different situation. Be the first one to encourage and inspire others, and motivate your team to believe in the possibility of success. However, know that taking this to an extreme could lead people to see you as naive and unrealistic; and just try to motivate, inspire, and encourage them when that happens!

Your positivity must be grounded in reality, not in a place of foolishness. Be optimistic in the face of adversity, but take a sober look at reality too, and always be truthful about it with your team.

Unfortunately, balance doesn't exist at some magical point on the spectrum between optimism and naivete. You simply have to feel it out. Your optimism should account for reality and consider the variables. Your tone should reflect realism so that you maintain credibility.

Strict versus Lenient

My best friend and I both played sports in high school. I liked the coaches who encouraged me and helped me grow. He liked the coaches who yelled in his face and pushed him to his limits.

There is no objectively right answer about how to strike a balance between strict and lenient because people react in different ways based on how they were raised and on their life experiences. You'll have to tailor your style to the individuals on your team, knowing what it takes to get the best out of each of them. Some people need support and coddling. Some people need strict rules and discipline. Dennis Rodman went to Las Vegas for a forty-eight-hour bender in the middle of the Chicago Bulls '97–'98 Championship season. Coach Phil Jackson approved it. Would you have let him go? Well, the Bulls won the Championship, and Rodman suited up for eighty games.

That said, a team that takes ownership likely doesn't need a leader to enforce strict rules and won't suffer if the rules are lenient. Where there is trust, you can course correct with either strictness or leniency when projects don't go perfectly according to plan.

Tip: Don't be a pushover. As you probably know by now, being a lovable leader doesn't mean letting the tough stuff go. When you care about your team members, you bravely face conflict and difficult conversations. You realign team members who go off track. You hold people accountable to their responsibilities. Precisely because you care, you stand your ground.

If you mistake being loved with being liked, you risk becoming a pushover, and the entire team suffers. When any member of the team disrespects the leader and gets away with it, it signals to the rest of the team a breakdown of respect and roles. The leader's job requires getting people to take ownership and action. Whether you are strict or lenient in how you accomplish that is a matter of personal style. However, your approach should always be supported by strong bonds with your team, substantial trust for one another, and deep respect. When you have this, you will be effective.

Praiseful versus Critical

As a leader, words are your most commonly used tool. Some people take the concept of being generous with praise too far and wind up walking around the office giving out compliments for anything anyone does. When you give too much praise, you diminish its impact because there is functionally no difference between big wins and common expectations. On the other hand, when you criticize too much, you cultivate a culture of fear and diminish people's motivation.

There is a delicate balance between praise and criticism, but I would offer that the ideal balance for a leader falls further toward praise than criticism. People want to feel important and to be appreciated. Similarly, people are far more likely to obsess over their shortcomings than to acknowledge, embrace, and recall their successes. Sometimes constructive criticism is important, useful, necessary; offer it in a spirit of good will and care so that it is as well-received as possible. Frame it in service of the other person's growth and as a product of your care.

LOVABLE LEADER'S CHEAT SHEET

To maintain balance in all aspects of my leadership, I will:

- Avoid going to extremes.

- Sometimes make unilateral decisions instead of collaborative ones.

- Sometimes need to assert control and sometimes need to let go.

- Ensure my optimism is not naive.

- Cater my strictness and leniency to individuals.

- Balance my praise and criticism.

- Seek to understand what I need to do to bring out the best in each individual.

11

THE MIRROR

You've now learned how to be in service of others. You've assumed responsibility, you carry the burden, and you acknowledge your privilege as a leader. Now, it's time to look in the mirror and take care of yourself.

IN THE fast-paced world of business, the competitive world of sports, or the perilous world of the military, there can be so many other more urgent matters to attend to than your own health. At least, that's how it feels. But physically, mentally, or emotionally weakened leadership can be a liability to your team's success.

In the big picture of your life, whatever you are working on is sufficiently less important than your physical, mental, and emotional health. And as a leader, you must prioritize your well-being. This means building in checks and balances to ensure that you take care of your own needs. Attention to your own health and wellness better equips you to help others when they need you, and it will build your stores of energy so that you are resilient. Fatigue, illness, and injury will be less likely. Your continued good health fuels you to continually tackle bigger and bigger challenges.

Attention to and care for your mental and emotional health will impact your ability to communicate, your motivation, your effectiveness in difficult situations, and the amount of satisfaction and pride you take in your work. Depression, overwhelm, burnout, unchecked frustration and anger, insecurity, and arrogance can all lead to catastrophic consequences in leadership roles.

Research from VitalSmarts, a leadership training company, has shown that "managers who clam up or blow up under pressure have teams with low morale; that are more likely to miss deadlines, budgets, and quality standards; and that act in ways that drive customers away." The research indicates that "at least 1 out of every 3 managers can't handle high-stakes, high-pressure situations," with "56% of people being more likely to shut down and stop participating." But none of this should come as a surprise. Our teams need us to be an example. They need us to guide them through times of uncertainty. As lovable leaders, we must tend to our mental health so that we can continue to create environments of care and trust that honor our commitment to safe travels. It's not an exaggeration to say that your potential as a leader is limited to how well you take care of yourself.

Leaders Need Love Too

Your job is to shoulder the burden, to carry the load, and to sacrifice for your team... but you have needs, as well. Build the kind of culture where feedback and recognition are given freely, even to you. And if you have a leader, make sure to acknowledge them too. Whether your manager is extraordinary or average, verbal validation can often mean the world to people and motivate them to be better leaders.

Make sure you have someone with whom you can talk and who gives you much-needed support. While it is nice to get it from your team, you do not expect it from them. Instead, find a mentor or friend who can be your sounding board and keep you grounded and feeling appreciated.

Be Proudly Incomplete

Always be dissatisfied with your current scope of knowledge and cultivate a burning desire to know more, to understand more. Admit and own your faults quickly and readily. Talk about your mistakes in real time and offer solutions to remedy situations, either through immediate action or things to focus on and steadily improve over time.

Let's look at how Walter, a sales manager at a mid-market technology company, handled a mistake. While one of his junior associates, Connie, was out on maternity leave, he reassigned her to a new sales team. Walter knew this was a smart business decision and an amazing growth opportunity for Connie. This new position gave her a brand-new territory to oversee and new team members to interact with. It also came with a small bump in pay. However, when Connie returned from maternity leave, she was less than enthusiastic. Having just spent several months enduring many sleepless nights and a full-time caretaker job, she had been looking forward to a return to familiarity. Furthermore, Walter had neglected to communicate the change to Connie himself, and instead, on her first day back, Connie found out from her old team that she was assigned to a new role. Connie approached Walter about the situation. Here was his response:

> Connie, I have a lot to apologize for. First of all, I should've been the one to tell you about the change of teams, and it's unacceptable that I put you in a position to find out the way that you did. You are an important part of this team and someone I have always been able to rely on. You deserved better than that from me. I am sincerely sorry. I can't undo that part, but I can do my best to make sure that you are set up for success moving forward.
>
> I also want to apologize for not talking to you about whether or not this change was even something you wanted. I didn't think about how it would make you feel coming back to a different role, because all that I thought about were the benefits. I know that this is a blind spot for me, and it's something that I am going to work on. In the meantime, I want to make sure that I fix this. I made a mistake in making this move without

talking to you. Can we talk about how we can either make this work for you or get you back into the role you were in previously, if that's what you would like? I'm also open to talking about other options.

You build trust with others by showing them your self-awareness and willingness to admit when you are wrong. People will have a deeper respect for you if they perceive that you operate with the keen understanding that you are imperfect. It further accentuates and adds weight to the times when you need to convince others that you are right. By admitting your mistakes and faults, you show people you are aware of them. When you propose solutions, you show people that you are willing to fix the problems. This communicates your commitment to consistent and ongoing improvement.

Be confident yet humble. Remember that it's okay to swagger from time to time. Intimately get to know your strengths and weaknesses. Ask for feedback. Aggressively track down your blind spots. Great leaders are always a work in progress; your growth will accelerate the more keenly aware of your strengths and weaknesses you can become.

When you feel let down

The disappointment of the team letting you down is one of the most difficult things you'll have to endure as a leader. When you put everything into your role and you believe in and trust your people, and they let you down, it can bring about many dark thoughts. You could find yourself wondering if you're any good as a leader. You might try to figure out where you went wrong. You may question everything.

There are two reactions that can help: 1) give yourself some space, and 2) take ownership. Whether or not you realize it, you're not perfect. We all make mistakes, and we're all learning as we go. That's how all of this works.

So, on the one hand, when things go wrong, give yourself some space to be imperfect. Allow for the possibility that you cannot control or fix everything. Every team is the product of multiple individuals working together, and even under the best circumstances, failure can happen. Realize this and allow for it. Regardless of how big the failure, it's likely not the end of the world.

Sometimes an individual will let you down. They might lie to you, go behind your back to betray you, or even sabotage a project. In any of these cases, only once you've given yourself some space are you ready to take ownership and improve wherever you can to see that it doesn't happen again. Keep your principles intact and stick to your own path of respect, trust, and care, knowing that a single person's behavior doesn't represent the entire team. Failure is not the time to beat yourself up. It's the time to give yourself some space then take ownership and get to work.

Tip: Beware the harshest critic. Who's the harshest critic in your world? Is it your boss? (*Why is he such a jerk?!*) Is it your parents? (*Ugh, why won't they just get off my back?!*) Or is it you? (*This isn't good enough. I can do better.*) If you are motivated and ambitious, your harshest critic is probably you. Holding yourself to your highest standard, being competitive with yourself, and pushing yourself to the limit are good things. But don't forget to take a deep breath and cut yourself some slack. Most things aren't truly important enough to lose sleep over. Since you are likely your own harshest critic, it's important that you confront yourself first and develop strategies for managing your own high expectations of yourself.

Therapy

In the same way that all humans should have a doctor they can consult regarding their physical health, everyone should have a therapist to consult regarding their mental health. For too long there has been a stigma against seeing mental health therapists, as if simply seeing one is evidence that someone is "crazy." This line of thinking is dangerous. There should be no shame at all in tending to your mental and emotional health, and doing so is not a sign of weakness.

Leaders are often under tremendous pressure, and therapy can often be one of the most effective methods of managing that pressure. In the absence of professional help, we can conjure up all manner of self-criticisms, self-doubt, anxieties, shame, and insecurities that take up space in our minds rent-free. A therapist can be exactly the right person to help you work through a challenging situation at the office or on the team. They can be the mental check for you to examine the evidence, consider an alternative point of view, or understand past trauma that led you to believe certain things or act in certain ways that undermine your current goals.

Leadership is a responsibility, a burden, and a privilege, and sometimes a therapist is the only person who can help you sort through your thoughts to tell these ideas apart. Your team is not there to be relief for your mental and emotional health; your therapist is. I advise you to find one as soon as possible, and find the cadence of speaking with them that makes the most sense, even if it's only every other month.

Meditation

Much in the same way that a therapist can help you manage the stress that leadership places on your mental and emotional health, the practice of mindfulness meditation can have a profoundly positive impact. Mindfulness meditation centers the experience of being present and attentive, usually by focusing on the breath. It is a process of slowing down and noticing your thoughts and feelings, allowing you to see them with a greater sense of awareness that is intended to be judgment-free.

Meditation is a valuable tool to have as a leader. It will help you in a variety of ways. Regularly practicing mindfulness meditation before difficult conversations with your team can help you detach from your automatic reactions and respond more thoughtfully. In high-stress situations, pausing to practice mindfulness can help you reset your emotions and reduce stress, even after only a few minutes of meditation. And as a leader, you are often under pressure to maintain intense focus for long periods of time. As a form of mental training, meditation can improve your focus.

Mentors

There is a pervasive narrative surrounding self-sufficiency. The motto of "pull yourself up by your bootstraps" either consciously or unconsciously conditions us not to ask for help. But is there any doubt that it is the collaborative spirit of humankind throughout time that has made nearly every great accomplishment possible? All substantial acts are generally created by people working together.

So, you should ask for help. Asking for help signals that you respect the other person as well as acknowledge their value and skill. It shows that you are humble enough to admit the limitations of your knowledge and that you trust the person you are asking for help by way of being vulnerable.

When you listen to someone's advice and then go on to use that advice, you validate that other person's worth, as well as give yourself the opportunity to learn and grow from new ideas.

Confronting the Monster Workaholic

Ambition, when left unchecked, can lead to workaholism. The longer you let this go on, the more it becomes a habit, and the more difficult it can be to break. For the sake of everyone's sanity and for the culture of work, we need to put workaholism to bed for good.

Workaholism, like any addiction, is the outgrowth of something that is, on its own, not a problem. There is nothing wrong with ambition. There is nothing wrong with hard work. There's not even anything wrong with long hours. But these are not examples of workaholism.

Let me say it differently.

There is nothing wrong with drinking an alcoholic beverage or two. There's not even anything wrong with getting drunk. There is, however, a problem when you cannot control it, and when it begins to negatively impact other areas of your life. Workaholism, like alcoholism or any other addiction, is characterized by its negative attributes and removal of a person's agency through compulsive and uncontrolled behavior.

As a leader, how and when you work is a signal to your team. You are always serving as an example. Consider that by engaging in a compulsive addiction to work that leaves you feeling burned out and unable to relax, you may be contributing to someone else on your team experiencing the same things. This is not how you create safe travels—and it's certainly not how you care—for your teammates or for yourself.

You must constantly be vigilant about your habits so that you foster your energy, passion, and ability to enjoy leisure time. Take time to rest, knowing that it will likely improve your focus and productivity at work. Plan for time off the clock, and set a good example for your team while giving yourself the space to recharge.

And if you see one of your team members developing workaholism, encourage them to take some time off, letting them know you are doing so because you want the best from them and for them.

Vacation, and Mental Health and Sick Days

When you are on vacation, be on vacation. Don't check email, don't check in with the team—reap the full benefits of your break. Always use your vacations to recharge and connect with yourself, those you care about, and the activities you enjoy outside work. Strictly enforce this policy for your team as well.

Also give yourself and any member of your team the freedom to ask for and take mental health days in the same way you would sick days. Care about your team in every way. Trust your team members, and when they say that they need the day off, believe that they do, without questioning them.

If any of your employees are sick, let them stay home. In fact, please suggest to them that they take their time to rest and get well. They will recover faster this way than if they were forced to begrudgingly and ineffectively work while ill. Granting them the time off is also a fairly easy way to show them that you care about their well-being and the well-being of your team.

If any of your employees or team members have a death in the family, no matter how close or distant to the immediate family, *let them take all the time off they need.*

Matters of life and death and family are bigger than work. Never forget that. No one on their deathbed wishes that they worked just a little bit more.

LOVABLE LEADER'S CHEAT SHEET

To take care of myself as a leader, I will:

- Give myself space to be imperfect.

- Take my mental and emotional health seriously.

- Continually invest in my own growth.

- Seek out mentors who will challenge me and keep me grounded.

- Take time off and vacations to avoid burnout.

CONCLUSION
LEADING UPWARD

WHEN THE topic of leadership comes up, most people tend to think of hierarchies—specifically, people tend to look to the person one up in the hierarchy for directions. However, in many organizations nowadays, the org chart may be flat. In some cases, businesses operate within a matrix structure, or possibly even a multimatrixed or honeycomb structure. In short, the levels aren't as clear as they once were.

This is probably a good thing. Leadership is *always* your responsibility, your burden, and your privilege. This applies to leading not only downward but also upward to your manager. Leading upward shares many of the same principles as effective top-down leadership. In fact, I would argue that you can apply all the principles in this book to managing upward. The biggest difference is obviously a shift in the power dynamic. While leaders higher in the org chart can appeal to their organizational status, leading upward cannot rest on that fallback position.

Here are some quick tips for the type of leadership where you are leading your peers or even your managers.

Trade Solutions for Inquiry

Among the most important things to do when leading upward is to trade solutions for inquiry. Stated differently, instead of going to your manager and asking for direction, be prepared to present your suggested actions or solutions. Then, open the door to collect their feedback. This is especially critical when dealing with a manager who is busy with a variety of other projects, tasks, or teams.

By presenting a well-thought-out option as a starting point, you alleviate your manager's responsibility to lead another initiative. It shows that you are proactive and take ownership over your role at the same time as you are open to their input.

Ask How You Could Have Done Better

Sometimes you may come prepared with a solution, possibly even objectively the best idea, but your manager still rejects it. When this happens, pinning the blame on your manager's short-sightedness would be very easy. You could even be angry at them.

I suggest that you approach the situation with a singular question: *How could I have done a better job presenting my case and achieving my objective?* Start by asking yourself this question, and then, if you have a good relationship with your manager, consider asking them directly. There is little value in assigning blame and standing in your righteousness. Instead, think about how you presented your position. Ask:

- *Was my idea clear and concise?* Perhaps you left out critical details, or maybe you included too many.

- *Was my idea that good?* We all tend to like our own ideas. After all, we came up with them. Use critical thinking to assess the validity of your idea.

- *Why might my manager be rejecting this idea?* Do the analysis. Try to figure it out.

The bottom line is that instead of blaming, which creates no additional forward movement, consider how you can use this lesson to improve. Each defeat is an opportunity to work on your skills of influence and persuasion. Take full ownership and move forward.

The Big Secret That's Hiding in Plain Sight

All the leadership advice in this book pertains to a single individual working in an organization. And it also applies to leadership in all areas of your life.

The lovable leadership framework is valuable for companies, for people coming out of college looking to grow their network, for people getting into politics, or really any human being on this planet who interacts with other human beings. (Hint: That's *all* of us.) You can learn these principles and let them permeate your behavior in all areas of your life.

Think about everything you've read and ask yourself: What if we all behaved as lovable leaders and we did it everywhere? What would a world with more care, trust, and safety look like?

Let's build a better world together.
Go forth and be lovable.

Lovingly,

JEFF GIBBARD

ACKNOWLEDGMENTS

THIS BOOK would not have been possible without the following people. I want to take a moment to acknowledge each of them.

Most importantly, my wife, Erica: This book is your book. I wrote it for you. It was inspired by you. It wouldn't have happened without you. You are my muse, my forever, my everything. You inspire me to be the best version of myself every day. I couldn't do what I do without you in my corner cheering me on. Being around you never lets me forget the importance of love in all things. That's why when I saw you move into a leadership role, I knew exactly what the title of this book would be. Thank you for helping me be the superhero I aspire to be. I love you.

My parents—Dad, Maryanne, Mom, Horace Burns, and Margaret Reilly: I am the canvas upon which each of you left your permanent brush strokes. I am thankful every day that I was lucky enough to be born into this family. I grew up in houses of love and respect, boundaries and freedoms. I see the world the way I do because of each of you. Thank you for inspiring so much of this book and for helping me to become the person I am.

My daughter (and any future children): Being a father is everything I had hoped it would be and more. You help me understand love in a new way, one that I couldn't have imagined until the day you arrived. I hope that I am every bit as good of a leader as I've described in these pages, but more than that, I hope to inspire you to grow up to be a lovable leader who will change the world. I love you with every cell in my body and with the force of one thousand exploding suns.

My close friends, family, and teammates—Jon Steiert, Jessica Smith, Jessica Rutkowski, Tim Eulie, Q. Xavier, Sarah Ohanesian, Parchelle Tashi, Natalie Miller, Matt Engler, Ellie Siegel, Julian Kam, and Bart Mroz: every one of you has contributed to my growth as a person. Some of you I had the opportunity and privilege to work with, some of you I had the opportunity to directly manage, and some of you I'm just lucky enough to call a friend or family member. I'm grateful to have had the opportunity to learn from all of you. Thank you.

Huge thanks to all of the authors, speakers, podcasters, and leaders I know (and some who I don't know personally) who inspire me: Yvonne Alston, Christopher Li, Jeff Harry, Tamsen Webster, Dorie Clark, Robbie Samuels, Leslie Ehm, Mitch Joel, Laura Gassner Otting, Brené Brown, Seth Godin, Simon Sinek, Adam Grant, Christina Blacken, Tony Chatman, Jeffrey Shaw, Ron Tite, Deb Gabor, Dr. George James, Mike Domitzr, Brian Fanzo, Scott Monty, Chris Brogan, Marc Pitman, Jeanette Bronée,

Phil M. Jones, Oren Klaff, Mike Michalowicz, Ann Shey-bani, John C. Maxwell, Robin Dreeke, Jocko Willink, Leif Babin, Chris Voss, Dale Carnegie, Donald Miller, Doug Sandler, Bob Burg, and Ryan Hawk.

The managers, clients, vendors, and partners I've had the good fortune to know, learn from, agree with, and disagree with—Jon Greenawalt, Betsy Johnson, Jay Devine, Vince Powers, Steve Loose, Wil Reynolds, Rand Fishkin, Jay Sullivan, Calvin Sullivan, William Sullivan, Richard Sullivan, Steve Robertson, and Steve Robinson: I've learned so much from watching each of you. Even when I disagreed with one of you, I learned something... including that I can be wrong. Thank you all for being an inspiration.

And all the bad managers, bad clients, backstabbers, and questionable human beings I've met along the way or heard about secondhand: You may be awful, but at least you gave me some fuel to write this book.

NOTES

Introduction: Call to Action

"Furthermore, it's estimated that..." State of the American Workplace
(Washington, DC: Gallup, 2017), gallup.com/workplace/
238085/state-american-workplace-report-2017.aspx.

"The Edelman Trust Barometer..." "2020 Edelman Trust Barometer,"
Edelman, January 19, 2020, edelman.com/trust-barometer.

"The survey shows 35%..." "Workplace Stress Continues to Mount,"
Korn Ferry, accessed May 31, 2021, kornferry.com/insights/
this-week-in-leadership/workplace-stress-motivation.

Chapter 1: The Lovable Leadership Mindset

"This entire scenario and the resultant..." Wikipedia, s.v. "Deontological ethics," en.wikipedia.org/wiki/Deontological_ethics.

Chapter 2: Care

"And anyone who has seen..." Brené Brown, "Listening to Shame,"
TED video, posted March 16, 2012, YouTube, 20:35, youtube.
com/watch?v=psN1DORYYV0.

"Robert Cialdini's seminal book..." Robert Cialdini, *Influence: The
Psychology of Persuasion* (New York: William Morrow, 1993).

"One episode, my guest..." "Mic Swap: Doug Sandler Interviews Jeff
Gibbard," in *Shareable*, podcast, episode 2, February 21, 2017,
9:00, shareablepodcast.com/2/.

"Everyone remembers something different…" Dale Carnegie, *How to Win Friends and Influence People* (New York: Pocket Books, 1981).

"Similarly, William James is quoted…" William James, "The deepest principle…," BrainyQuotes, brainyquote.com/quotes/william_james_125466.

"Three powerful words:…" Jeff Haden, "With Just 3 Words, Michael Jordan Taught Mike Kryzewski a Powerful Lesson in Emotional Intelligence," Inc., inc.com/jeff-haden/with-just-3-words-michael-jordan-taught-mike-krzyzewski-a-powerful-lesson-in-emotional-intelligence.html. Emphasis in original.

Chapter 3: Trust

"In this article, Chris shares…" Chris Brogan, "Apologize Immediately," Chris Brogan Media, June 15, 2006, chrisbrogan.com/apologize-immediately/.

"And while I'm sure someone…" Mike Monteiro, *Ruined by Design: How Designers Destroyed the World, and What We Can Do to Fix It* (Fresno: Mule Design, 2019), Kindle.

"He draws his bow…" Joss Whedon, dir., *The Avengers: Age of Ultron* (Burbank: Walt Disney Studios, 2015).

"He even went so far as…" Wil Reynolds, "Rules of the Road: CEO Swap with 'Fish' Rand Fishkin," Seer, seerinteractive.com/blog/rules-of-the-road-ceo-swap-with-fish-rand-fishkin/.

"That said, as the leader,…" Rand Fishkin, "Wil, Here's Some Things I Think Are Holding Seer Back (And Some Things That Are Making Seer Amazing)," Seer, seerinteractive.com/blog/wil-heres-some-things-i-think-are-holding-seer-back-and-some-things-that-are-making-seer-amazing/.

Chapter 4: Safe Travels

"According to the Harvard Business Review *article…"* Laura Sherbin and Ripa Rashid, "Diversity Doesn't Stick without Inclusion," *Harvard Business Review*, February 1, 2017, hbr.org/2017/02/diversity-doesnt-stick-without-inclusion.

"Think of conflict as similar…" "Kintsugi: The Art of Embracing
Damage," Nerdwriter1, YouTube video, posted May 30, 2014,
4:33, youtube.com/watch?v=lT55_u8URU0.
"As a philosophy, Kintsugi…" Wikipedia, s.v. "Kintsugi," en.wiki
pedia.org/wiki/Kintsugi.
"In it, a small challenge…" Wikipedia, s.v. "The Prisoner's Dilemma,
Generalized Form," en.wikipedia.org/wiki/Prisoner%27s_
dilemma#Generalized_form.
"'Productive conflict' is a term…" Liane Davey, *The Good Fight: Use
Productive Conflict to Get Your Team and Organization Back on
Track* (Vancouver: Page Two Books, 2019).

Chapter 5: Your Most Important Tool
"To take a deep dive with this,…" Robert Cialdini, *Influence: The
Psychology of Persuasion* (New York: William Morrow, 1993);
Pre-Suasion: Channeling Attention for Change (New York: Simon
& Schuster, 2016).

Chapter 6: The Destination
"Studies have shown that…" See, for example, Stefano I. Di
Domenico and Richard M. Ryan, "The Emerging Neuro-
science of Intrinsic Motivation: A New Frontier in Self-
Determination Research," *Frontiers in Human Neuroscience* 11
(2017): 145, ncbi.nlm.nih.gov/pmc/articles/PMC5364176/; E.L.
Deci, R. Koestner, and R.L. Ryan, "A Meta-Analytic Review of
Experiments Examining the Effects of Extrinsic Rewards on
Intrinsic Motivation," *Psychological Bulletin* 125, no. 6 (1999):
627–68, pubmed.ncbi.nlm.nih.gov/10589297/.
"And this is clearly something worth…" Chris Musser, "One
Employee Question That Leaders Can't Afford to Ignore,"
Gallup, September 27, 2019, gallup.com/workplace/267014/
one-employee-question-leaders-afford-ignore.aspx.
"I like to recall a scene…" Peter Weir, dir., *Dead Poets Society*
(Burbank: Buena Vista Pictures Distribution, 1989).

"He quotes a poem..." Walt Whitman, "O Me! O Life!," Poetry
Foundation, poetryfoundation.org/poems/51568/o-me-o-life.

"Jim Collins coined a term..." Jim Collins and Jerry Porras, *Built
to Last: Successful Habits of Visionary Companies* (New York:
Harper Business Essentials, 2002).

"'When you step out...'" Ira Boudway, "The Five Pillars of Popovich,"
Bloomberg Businessweek, January 10, 2018, bloomberg.com/
news/features/2018-01-10/the-five-pillars-of-gregg-popovich.

Chapter 7: The Map

"We can look to the first..." John Favreau, dir., *Iron Man* (Hollywood:
Paramount Pictures, 2008).

"You need a clear strategy document..." My Strategy Brief template
can help with this. Find it at docs.google.com/document/
d/1ovBjQ5B9a_QAB65YqeMHpcdhHljFHKL8gfSxBzWDLhc/
edit. The following articles on my site may also help, for additional context: "The Friction Ladder: What Causes Inter-
personal Problems at Work and How to Fix It," jeffgibbard.
com/friction-ladder/; "Work, Love, and Language," jeffgibbard
.com/work-love-and-language/; "Your High-Performing-Team-
Squad-Family," jeffgibbard.com/your-high-performing-team-
squad-family/; and "The Leadership Golden Rule," jeffgibbard.
com/the-leadership-golden-rule/.

"In his book Good to Great,*..."* Jim Collins, *Good to Great: Why
Some Companies Make the Leap...And Others Don't* (New York:
Harper Business, 2001).

Chapter 8: The Journey

"This quote is typically attributed..." "Everybody is a Genius..."
Quote Investigator, quoteinvestigator.com/2013/04/06/
fish-climb/.

"Love told Vaynerchuk that..." "#AskGaryVee 318 | Kevin Love,"
Gerald's Views (blog), February 5, 2020, YouTube video,
1:00:06, gerald-pilcher.com/askgaryvee-318-kevin-love/.

"*Once you fall into the pattern...*" Mark R. Lepper, David Greene, and Richard E. Nisbett, "Undermining Children's Intrinsic Interest with Extrinsic Reward: A Test of the 'Overjustification' Hypothesis," *Journal of Personality and Social Psychology* 28, no. 1 (1973): 129–37, web.mit.edu/curhan/www/docs/Articles/ 15341_Readings/Motivation/Lepper_et_al_Undermining_ Childrens_Intrinsic_Interest.pdf.

Chapter 10: The Balance

"*According to a study...*" This was shown in a study known as the "Overjustification Hypothesis": "Subjects agreed to engage in the target activity in order to obtain an extrinsic reward; ...the results supported the prediction that subjects in the expected-award condition would show less subsequent intrinsic interest in the target activity." See Daniel Wheatley, "Autonomy in Paid Work and Employee Subjective Well-being," *Work and Occupations* 44, no. 3 (2017): 296–328, doi.org/10.1177/07308884176 97232.

Chapter 11: The Mirror

"*The research indicates that...*" "The Manager Effect: 1 Out of 3 Managers Can't Handle High-Stakes Situations and as a Result, Their Teams Are Less Successful," VitalSmarts, press release, November 6, 2018, vitalsmarts.com/press/2018/11/the-manager-effect-1-out-of-3-managers-cant-handle-high-stakes-situations-and-as-a-result-their-teams-are-less-successful/.

FURTHER READING

THIS LIST is of books I strongly recommend you read or listen to in service of becoming a better leader and a more capable human being. (Links to these and more can be found at loveableleader.com/books.)

Brown, Brené. *Daring Greatly.* New York: Avery, an imprint of Penguin Random House, 2012.

Brown, Jennifer. *How to be an Inclusive Leader.* Oakland: Berrett-Koehler Publishers, 2019

Carnegie, Dale. *How to Win Friends and Influence People.* New York: Pocket Books, 1998.

Cialdini, Robert. *Influence: The Psychology of Persuasion.* New York: Harper Business, 2006.

Clark, Timothy R. *The 4 Stages of Psychological Safety.* Oakland: Berrett-Koehler Publishers, 2020.

Clear, James. *Atomic Habits: An Easy and Proven Way to Build Good Habits and Break Bad Ones.* New York: Avery, 2018.

Collins, Jim. *Good to Great: Why Some Companies Make the Leap... And Others Don't.* New York: Harper Business, 2001.

Collins, Jim, and Jerry Porras. *Built to Last: Successful Habits of Visionary Companies.* New York: Harper Business, 2002.

Davey, Liane. *The Good Fight: Use Productive Conflict to Get Your Team and Organization Back on Track*. Vancouver: Page Two Books, 2019.

DiAngelo, Robin. *White Fragility: Why It's So Hard for White People to Talk About Racism*. Boston: Beacon Press, 2018.

Fuller, Pamela, and Mark Murphy. *The Leader's Guide to Unconscious Bias*. New York: Simon & Schuster, 2020.

Greene, Robert. *The Laws of Human Nature*. New York: Penguin Books, 2018.

Kendi, Ibram X. *How To Be Anti-Racist*. New York: One World, 2019.

Klaff, Oren. *Flip the Script: Getting People to Think Your Idea Is Their Idea*. New York: Portfolio, 2019.

———. *Pitch Anything: An Innovative Method for Presenting, Persuading, and Winning the Deal*. New York: McGraw Hill, 2011.

Lewis, John. *Carry On*. New York: Grand Central Publishing, 2021.

Maxwell, John C. *Leadershift: 11 Essential Changes Every Leader Must Embrace*. New York: HarperCollins, 2019.

Oluo, Ijeoma. *So You Want to Talk About Race*. New York: Seal Press, 2018.

Perry, Rhodes, and John Lewis. *Belonging at Work*. Portland: RPC Academy Press, 2018.

Saad, Layla. *Me and White Supremacy: Combat Racism, Change the World, and Become a Good Ancestor*. Naperville, IL: Sourcebooks, 2020.

Sinek, Simon. *Leaders Eat Last: Why Some Teams Pull Together and Others Don't*. Rev. ed. New York: Portfolio, 2017.

Sun Tzu. *Art of War*. New York: Chartwell Books, 2012.

Voss, Chris. *Never Split the Difference: Negotiation as if Your Life Depended on It*. New York: Harper Business, 2016.

Willink, Jocko, and Leif Babin. *Extreme Ownership: How U.S. Navy Seals Lead and Win*. Rev. ed. New York: St. Martin's Press, 2017.

———. *The Dichotomy of Leadership*. New York: St. Martin's Press, 2018.

Wong, Alice, ed. *Disability Visibility*. New York: Vintage Books, 2020.

ABOUT
THE AUTHOR

JEFF GIBBARD is a strategist, consultant, speaker, and trainer, and founder of The Superhero Institute, a training and development company that shows people how to unlock the potential of leadership, communication, strategy, and enduring growth. He is also the host of the popular *Shareable* and *Rogue* podcasts, and a board member of both Pathways to Housing PA and Council for Relationships.

After earning his MBA in 2008 and spending a decade working as a social media and content marketing strategist, Jeff took a hard pivot in 2019 to help humanize the online world, inspire the next wave of extraordinary leaders, and give every human being access to the tools and training they need to be more strategic, thoughtful, and effective.

THE LOVABLE LEADER
CALL TO ACTION

BE PART of the movement to fix our broken culture through Lovable Leadership. Here a few ways you can help:

Write a review: Book reviews are a quick way for you to help this book to climb the charts and encourage people to pick up a copy. If you enjoyed this book, tell people why in a review on Amazon. Your review may just help us create one more Lovable Leader in the world.

Share the book: Whether you buy a copy or share yours, what's important is spreading the ideas of trust, respect, and kindness as the path for building great teams and healing our culture of work.

Bulk copies: If you feel that an entire team would benefit from reading *The Lovable Leader*, we have excellent offers available for orders of ten or more, including physical copies and e-books. For details, and to order, visit lovableleader.com.

- **Hire me to speak:** I am passionate about speaking with audiences of all sizes, online and in person, to help people grow into the Lovable Leaders they're meant to be. For more information, visit jeffgibbard.com/speaking.

  Consulting: Companies hire me to design effective strategies for growth, including brand, leadership, marketing, and sales. Through purpose, creativity, and critical thinking, I help organizations become the best versions of themselves. To start the conversation, go to: jeffgibbard.com/work-with-jeff/.

- **Content:** From blogs to podcasts, videos, and discussions, I create content regularly. Often inspired by questions from clients, friends, and peers, I am always looking for ways to explore interesting topics and provide valuable insights. Visit jeffgibbard.com/content.

- **The Superhero Institute:** This coaching-certification program specializes in teaching you how to unleash human potential in service of making the world a safer, kinder, more equitable place. To learn more, visit: superheroinstitute.org.

  Connect with me: If you want to connect with me on social media, go here: jgibbard.com/connect.